LOST BOYS

AND THE MOMS
WHO LOVE THEM

LOST BOYS

AND THE MOMS WHO LOVE THEM

Encouragement and Hope for Dealing
with Your Wayward Son

‖ MELODY CARLSON ‖ HEATHER KOPP ‖
‖ LINDA CLARE ‖

WATERBROOK
PRESS

LOST BOYS AND THE MOMS WHO LOVE THEM
PUBLISHED BY WATERBROOK PRESS
2375 Telstar Drive, Suite 160
Colorado Springs, Colorado 80920
A division of Random House, Inc.

All Scripture quotations, unless otherwise indicated, are taken from the *New King James Version.* Copyright © 1982 by Thomas Nelson, Inc. Used by permission. All rights reserved. Other scriptures taken from the *Holy Bible, New International Version®*. NIV®. Copyright © 1973, 1978, 1984 by International Bible Society. Used by permission of Zondervan Publishing House. All rights reserved.

"Listen, Lord," "An Encouraging Word," "A Prodigal Prayer," and "I Wasn't Prepared for a Prodigal" are excerpted from *Prodigals and Those Who Love Them* by Ruth Bell Graham, copyright 1999, and are used by permission of Baker Book House Company.

Name and details in some anecdotes and stories have been changed to protect the identities of the persons involved.

ISBN 1-57856-483-2

Copyright © 2002 by Melody Carlson, Heather Kopp, and Linda Clare

Library of Congress Cataloging-in-Publication Data
Carlson, Melody.
    Lost boys and the moms who love them : encouragement and hope for dealing with your wayward son / Melody Carlson, Heather Kopp, Linda Clare.—1st ed.
      p. cm.
    ISBN 1-57856-483-2
      1. Parenting—Religious aspects—Christianity. 2. Mothers—Religious life.
3. Sons—Religious life. I. Kopp, Heather Harpham, 1964– II. Clare, Linda.
III. Title.

BV4529 .C42 2001
248.8'431—dc21

                2001046636

Printed in the United States of America
2002—First Edition

10 9 8 7 6 5 4 3 2 1

TO OUR BOYS:

Gabe, Luke, Noah, Nathan, Chris, Nathan, and Tim

LOVE,

Your Moms

CONTENTS

Acknowledgments

To our sons, all of whom were willing to have their stories told here in the hopes that they might help others. Thank you so much! We are so proud of every one of you. Without your cooperation and support, we could not have written this book.

We want to offer special thanks to the dozens of mothers who were so willing to share their stories with us. Your courage and honesty will deeply touch many moms who read these pages.

Finally, heartfelt thanks to our editor, Traci Mullins of Eclipse Editorial Services, for her constant encouragement, great editing skills, and her dedication to making this book the best it could be.

A NOTE FROM THE AUTHORS

It seems like just yesterday that your son was a precious, precocious little boy who loved to give you kisses and talk with you about everything. So when and how did he turn into a problem teenager who brushes away hugs, resists your advice, and views you as the enemy?

Perhaps it began with a little back talk or moodiness or simply a change in his hairstyle or musical tastes. Or maybe he dropped out of basketball or brought home an F in algebra. Perhaps he even pierced or tattooed some part of his body (that same precious body you've protected and nurtured all his life!). At any rate, he seems to have lost his moral and spiritual compass. And the more "lost" he becomes, the more lost you feel.

We understand how painful it is when a son rebels or otherwise strays from the good and happy path we had in mind for him. We, too, have sons who, though raised in Christian homes with loving parents, have caused us years of trouble and heartache. "Trouble" has included everything from drinking parties to skipping school to criminal behavior. "Heartache" is a big word for a lot of bad feelings: guilt, shame, fear, confusion, panic.

Maybe you feel at your wits' end with nowhere to turn for compassion and support. Maybe you've spent many sleepless nights worrying about your son's physical and spiritual welfare. Probably you feel embarrassed and judged and possibly even rejected by your social or religious community.

Whatever you're going through, we want you to know that you are not alone and that there is a reason to have hope.

In an effort to help and encourage moms like you, we teamed up to write *Lost Boys*. We decided not to write yet another "how to fix your child in twelve easy steps" book (because we know better). Instead, we want to help you cope with the jumble of doubts and fears that plague the mothers of wayward sons. We'll introduce you to lots of other moms who walk the same road you do, who offer empathy, comfort, and helpful counsel on dealing with common dilemmas.

Each of the twelve sections in *Lost Boys* opens with an introduction written by one of us. This is where you get to know us and something about the personal struggles that compelled us to write this book. Amazingly, all of our sons gave their permission for us to write about them, knowing that in sharing some of the intimate details of our stories we might help other mothers to help their sons.

It is our sincere hope that you will receive this book as an invitation to laugh and cry with moms who care and understand. May it be a comfort to you on those nights when your son has missed his curfew—again. And may it finally lead you into prayer with a loving Father, who will never lose sight of, much less give up on, any of his lost sons.

> With our love and prayers,
> Melody, Heather, and Linda

Part I

WHAT WAS...

HE WAS JUST A LITTLE BOY

HEATHER

When Noah was four or five, I experienced every mom's worst nightmare. I lost him in the shopping mall. One minute he was whining while I looked at kids' clothes in JCPenney, and the next he was nowhere to be found.

I began to check under clothes racks and then scanned the toy department. When there was still no sign of him after five minutes, I started to get those fluttering feelings of panic in my belly, which, if you've ever misplaced your child in a public place, you can easily remember.

I alerted a store clerk, who in turn alerted mall security. I tried not to cry as they put out Noah's description and began a check, store by store: *Blond, blue eyes, five years old but the size of a seven-year-old, wearing a striped green-and-white shirt and jeans.*

After an agonizing twenty minutes, a cashier in a small shop recognized my son. But not because he was crying, looking lost, or asking for help. In fact, he was diligently walking down the length of the mall, patiently peering into store after store, looking for me.

When we were reunited, I grabbed him, hugged him, and tearfully exclaimed, "You must have been so scared!"

He squirmed loose, explaining that he wasn't scared at all. He was never really lost. He just couldn't find me.

That's Noah for you.

These days Noah is not exactly worried about losing sight of me. In fact, you might say that this has become his goal. I'm sure you've noticed it too. At age five, your son wants to know where his mother is. By age ten, he isn't terribly worried about it. After age fourteen or so, separation from you becomes his main objective.

I've never liked the word "lost" when used in the Christian sense. Calling people "lost" seems insulting, even if they are "lost" in that they haven't "found" Jesus. And calling my teenager lost is not something I do to his face. But it is how I might describe my son these days. Lost—in the sense that he can't stay off dope without weekly drug tests. Lost—in the sense that he doesn't know who he is or where he's going spiritually.

Maybe your son is lost in a very different way. Maybe it's depression, violence, school problems, or alcohol that has him on a path so far from where you wish he were. There are a lot of ways for boys to be lost. Trouble is, when they're teenagers, there's no one around to alert security. And their description matches millions of other boys just like them.

Of course, a lot of our sons don't think they're lost at all. And maybe they're right. Maybe it's we moms who are lost. After all, we're the ones who had an ideal destination in mind for our boys and thought we knew how to get them there. And now it's we who feel spun around and blindfolded, no longer certain where we are or what went wrong. It's probably a universal principle: Once your baby—no matter how old he is—is lost, so are you.

One recent night Noah went out with some friends who seem to be alternately Christians and ruffians, depending on the weekend. Unlike them, Noah is being tested for drug use every Monday. This way he has no choice, no temptation, no dilemma. Deep down, I think he likes it that way.

The next morning I asked Noah how it went the night before, what they did. He said it was okay. Except for the part where everybody else got high before the movie and then again after the movie while he waited outside the car.

I told him I was sorry. And I was proud of him.

"But God spoke to me," he announced.

"Really?" (This is not typical.)

"Yeah," he said. "While I was standing around outside waiting for those guys to get high, I saw a double rainbow."

He wasn't really able to articulate what God seemed to be saying through the double rainbow, but I wasn't going to push. I reached up to ruffle his hair, and, surprisingly, he let me. Then he trotted off to the shower, a little boy inside a man-size body.

I kept thinking about that double rainbow all day. Maybe it was God's way of saying to my Noah, "Hey, you. Look at this cool rainbow. There's beauty in life I don't want you to miss. And no amount of dope will make it more beautiful."

And maybe Noah's telling me about it was God's way of saying to me, "Remember my promises. No matter how far he wanders away from you, he's never out of my sight."

Today, at eighteen, my son still seems lost to me. Almost every day I ask, How did we end up here? How did we go from lost in the mall to lost in life? From potty training to urine samples?

I'm sure you've asked yourself the same question time and again: How did this happen? He was just right here beside me. He was just a little boy...

It's likely you'll never fully know the answer to this question. But in the meantime, take comfort in knowing that with God, lost is not the same as hopeless. Lost is not the same as gone forever. Lost is simply what you are on your way to being found.

———

Be patient with boys—you are dealing with soul stuff.

ELBERT HUBBARD II

You Did What?

Karen lives in a small town where everyone knows everything about everybody. Her twelve-year-old, Cameron, had experienced the usual childhood scrapes, but she'd always considered him a pretty good kid— that is, until he did something that really threw her for a loop. She didn't know what to think or how to react. Was it just a childhood prank or a sign of something more?

C ameron's not perfect. But he gets average and better grades, seems to get along okay with his teachers and friends, and for the most part seems fairly responsible. I'll admit I expect a lot of him. Being a single mom and working full time isn't easy. And I feel guilty that I neglect him sometimes. But Cameron's been a good sport, and for the most part I'm really pretty proud of him. Maybe that's part of my problem now.

You see, I got a phone call from Cameron's middle school, asking me to come in to see the principal. No details or anything, but it sounded kind of serious. Well, it's not easy to just tell my manager that I have to leave work to go to my son's school, but fortunately we were having a slow afternoon at the store. So I hurried on over to see what was up. At least the school secretary had assured me Cameron was okay since my first conclusion was that he'd been hurt and I needed to take him to the hospital for stitches. We've done that before.

So, anyway, I get to the school, and I start thinking Cameron's done something wrong. He's in trouble. And then suddenly it's as if I'm in trouble too. I mean, I feel just like I'm in junior high again and getting called into the principal's office for smoking in the bathroom. My heart starts racing. I keep telling myself this is completely ridiculous, but by the time I get to Mr. Byron's office, my hands are clammy, and I feel slightly sick to my stomach. "What's the problem?" I ask, trying to hide my jitters.

The principal clears his throat as if it's not easy to say this. "We have a busload of witnesses, Cameron's classmates, who claim that Cameron exposed himself on the way home from school today."

Well, I'm almost speechless. I'm thinking: No way. No way would Cameron do something like this. Something this stupid and sordid. "Exposed himself?" I repeat dumbly.

Then Mr. Byron goes into the whole ugly story of how Cameron removed his pants and showed his rear end to a busload of kids. And for some reason I'm relieved to hear it was just his "rear end," but I'm not even sure why. Then I'm informed that Cameron is suspended and may be charged with sexual harassment, and somehow I manage to make it out of there without breaking into tears. I'm humiliated.

By the time I get home, I'm absolutely livid. I find Cameron playing a video game, as if he's oblivious to this whole nasty mess he's created. And as it turns out, he almost is. The bus driver just dropped him off without saying a word (as it turns out, the bus driver saw nothing). But when I tell Cameron where I've been and what I know and how much trouble he's in, he gets pretty defiant and defensive.

"I was just mooning them, Mom," he says with what I think is a cocky attitude. "I saw it in this video I watched at Aunt Kim's last weekend. It's no big deal."

I proceed to tell him loudly that it is a big deal, that he might have to go to court, that the whole town is probably talking about it by now, and what kind of movies does Aunt Kim let him watch anyway? I rant and rage for a while, and finally I notice his cockiness has disappeared, and I spy a couple of tears streaking down a freckled cheek. Now I feel horrible. I know I'm handling this all wrong. I try to settle down, and then I ask him why he did it. He just says, "I don't know."

Fortunately the school didn't press charges. But the principal sent an official-looking letter explaining how this is a very serious matter and how behavior like this could result in serious consequences. And I'm informed that a copy of this letter will remain in Cameron's file.

So now I'm trying to figure it all out. Was this some desperate cry for attention from my son? Is it because I'm a single mom and Cameron doesn't have a good male role model around? Will my son grow up to become a sexual deviant? Or was it just a childish prank? Should I get him counseling? Or maybe I need counseling. And if we need counseling, how will I pay for it? I've already asked some friends for advice, and some act like it's no big deal and tell me just to forget it, but others say it's a sign of deeper trouble. And I just don't know. To be honest, I've always been kind of proud of my son. I always tell people how mature he is, how he's such a great friend and helper to me. Now I feel a little ashamed of him, and I'm ashamed that I feel ashamed. I keep telling myself to lighten up, that it's just one stupid incident. But at the same time I'm also afraid. What if he does something like this again? What if he does something worse?

I think the bottom line (funny I should use that phrase) is that Cameron needs to know I love him no matter what. And I need to remind him of all he's done that makes me proud. And I need to let him know I forgive him. And if something else happens, well, we'll just deal with it. And in the meantime, I've told my sister that she's to monitor what the boys watch at her house!

—————

Children have more need of models than of critics.

JOSEPH JOUBERT

Everything's Backward

Nancy and Anthony have three children and live in a quiet residential neighborhood. For the past few years, their son Marcus has been giving them trouble. He's withdrawn, angry, hostile. But Nancy's real concern is that her relationship with Marcus is rapidly deteriorating. She misses so much the little boy he used to be. They used to be friends, but now she feels like she's his worst enemy. Marcus accuses her of nitpicking at him. Nancy knows he's probably right. But can she stop?

When you're a mom with a teenage boy, all your impulses are wrong. You can just count on it.

Nothing you do seems right to your son. You say everything wrong. You're strict when you should have been lenient. You hug him at the wrong time. You have the wrong opinion when it comes to anything to do with his clothes, music preferences, or movie tastes. It's as if you used to have a job being his mom, but now your job is to be a nag, a worrier, the most "wrong" person in his world.

My son Marcus is probably no worse than a lot of other boys. But he's making me crazy. It used to be that we had fun together, played games at night, watched *Jeopardy* and kept score with each other. Marcus is very smart. But these days he doesn't want anything to do with me. He comes home, shuts his bedroom door, and stays in his room unless I bang on the door loud enough for him to hear over the music that I'm calling him for dinner.

I'm just trying to figure out where it all changed and what I'm supposed to do now. He's sixteen. It's so hard to discipline him when he breaks the house rules. If I ground him, he just leaves anyway. And if I take away his car, his friends have plenty of cars. And if I try to smell his breath for alcohol, he calls me a Nazi. My husband, Anthony, is not faring any better. He's also at the bottom of Marcus's list of people who should be allowed to live.

Marcus used to be this straight-laced kid who wore polo shirts and kept his hair really short. Then he started to wear ratty clothes and grow his hair long. He claims that I don't approve of anything about him. That's not true. But I guess I do nag, and I do criticize a lot of things. And I did quit forcing him to go to church because his grungy clothes embarrassed me.

I know what I really need to do is try harder to let Marcus know I like him. But it's hard. I miss the little boy he used to be like you'd miss a whole different person. It's like he's just gone...

It's hard to stop saying negative things to this new Marcus when I'm always feeling dismayed about his choices. Maybe part of the trick is to do everything the opposite of what I feel I should do (since I'm always wrong). When I want to advise him about the way life really works, I probably need to ask his advice about something instead. When I want to say, "What are you wearing?!" I should probably say nothing. When I want to criticize his hair or his friends, I probably should compliment something else.

Speaking of hair, Marcus dyed his blond hair red last night. Not carrot red, but a dark cherry cola. There was a day when I felt terribly threatened by any change he made in his appearance. When he got his ear pierced at age twelve, I nearly had a heart attack. But last night we stood in the middle of Target and looked at the colors of dye, and his little sister helped him pick out a cherry cola. I could tell Marcus was shocked that I went along, especially when I paid for the dye.

When we got home, he and his sister were laughing and having a good time putting the dye on his hair in the bathroom. I was panicking, thinking about what a mess they were going to make. I knocked on the bathroom door, and they let me in. They both looked at me as if they knew I was about to get upset. I ended up not saying anything about how they were doing it or the mess they were making. I told Marcus that he probably should dye his eyebrows a little so they'd match.

Some advice he still takes. And you know what? Cherry cola looks good on him. It really does.

I Was Just...

HEATHER

I was just taking home videos of him wobbling down
the sidewalk on his first bike;
now I hear him screeching out of the driveway too fast
in his beat-up car.

I was just watching Scooby Doo with him on Saturday
mornings;
now I can't get him to stop watching MTV.

I was just posting his crayon drawings on the fridge;
now I'm posting the notice we got in the mail for his
next court date.

I was just trying to teach him to drink from a "sippy"
cup;
now I'm sniffing his breath to see if he's been drinking
beer again.

I was just washing his hair with baby shampoo, afraid
I'd get some in his eyes;
now my own are filled with tears.

I was just remembering...

And Tigger Too

Gary and Kim Brown worked hard to raise their children as well as to build a thriving construction business in Arizona. They golfed with executives and played tennis with celebrities. Their three girls were all bright and talented. But Gary longed for a son. The Browns adopted Bert as a toddler and thought they had the perfect family. But Kim recalls that no amount of resources helped as Bert began to get into trouble.

When Bert became part of our family, times were good—we'd just installed a lighted tennis court on the side of the house. My husband's construction business has been successful—we've been blessed in that way. I was delighted to have another little one, but I wasn't prepared for all the care and attention our new son would need.

In a photo of Bert taken shortly after he arrived, he's wearing this enormous cowboy hat—and all I see is this incredibly handsome kid, ready to take on the world. He was the cutest little boy I'd ever seen. All our girls have light hair and eyes, and they instantly adored their new little brother with his chestnut mop and huge brown eyes. By the second week, though, we'd nicknamed him "Tigger" because of the way he bounced from one thing to the next.

Bert's rambunctious behavior caught me off guard. Instead of the predictable schedule I'd enjoyed with my daughters, I was run ragged trying to keeping up with our little Tigger. He was adorable and maddening at the same time, refusing to nap, even waking up in the night to ask Gary and me if we wanted to play. We tried a lot of things, but the rocking chair worked best. He'd climb into my lap, and we'd rock and sing "Jesus Loves Me" until he nodded off.

By the time he was six, he still rarely slept for more than a few hours at a time. He couldn't sit still. Bert wasn't naughty on purpose, just very inquisitive. It took the whole family to keep up with his boundless energy. A doctor prescribed Ritalin for Bert's hyperactivity—in those days medication was not as widely used as it is now. It helped some, but our son seesawed between lethargy and frenetic agitation.

When the economy took a downturn, Bert was just starting school. Gary was forced to go as far as Texas to find work. He was away during the week and flew home on the weekends. Bert seemed lost. I enrolled our son in an exclusive day school, hoping it would help him with his social and academic skills. He was already showing signs of being a little behind.

Bert was a sensitive boy, and I think his own energy overwhelmed him at times. The many lights and sounds in the classroom made him irritable. He'd act out or get upset over very small things. If the glue didn't hold on his construction-paper project, he'd upend his chair and stomp out. Kids would tease him about his poor reading skills, and he'd punch the wall. The teacher began to call more and more frequently: Bert did this or Bert couldn't handle it today. I was getting more frustrated.

At home his behavior wasn't much better. The girls and I were used to his outbursts and his short attention span. But his dad had a harder time adjusting. The boy Gary always dreamed would love sports had trouble with coordination. Getting Bert to pay attention was difficult. By age twelve Tigger was a sullen, brooding ball of energy.

Gary and I sought the best treatments available. We paid plenty to try to help our son. I consulted expert after expert, hoping we'd find the key to unlock Bert's potential. Like a typical adolescent, he resented the psychologists, psychiatrists, and behavior-modification specialists. He'd deliberately play dumb at the sessions or just sit there, jiggling one nervous foot, practically daring the "shrinks," as he called them, to tell him he was crazy. His self-esteem was nonexistent, and each day was a struggle.

Somehow we all made it through to Bert's high-school years. He attended school with the children of senators and wealthy families, and he began to hang out around kids with high-profile last names. Before I knew it, Bert managed to get into trouble.

He had his driver's license, which he was really proud of. Some of his buddies—these kids drove new Corvettes and Mercedes to school—thought it would be fun to drag race down a main street. While showing off for these silver-spoon kids, Bert clipped the curb in my car and bounced it into another kid's sports car. Our car was totaled, and now Bert had more trouble than just paying attention in school. His license was suspended, and he received fines and probation.

That incident sent me into depression. I became terrified that Bert would end up hurting someone or killing himself. The kid could barely read, and I was sure he'd never make it through high school. All the money in the world wasn't enough to help him. For months, it seemed, I stayed in bed most of the time and cried.

I felt like staying there forever, hating myself, blaming myself for Bert's problems. But I couldn't forget that cute little boy in the big cowboy hat, the one we called Tigger. The little boy I rocked and sang to when he couldn't sleep at night was still in there somewhere. Slowly I began to focus on Bert's strengths instead of his weaknesses.

Bert eventually got a GED and has a job working alongside his dad in construction. He didn't turn out to be the son I assumed I'd get—quiet and intellectual, good at everything he tries. But he's funny and bright in his own way. Remembering that wonderful little boy, I find it's easier to turn Tigger over to God and to love him as deeply as a mother can.

Listen, Lord

RUTH BELL GRAHAM

Listen, Lord
a mother's praying
low and quiet:
listen, please.
Listen what her tears
are saying,
see her heart
upon its knees;
lift the load
from her bowed shoulders
till she sees
and understands,
You, Who hold
the worlds together,
hold her problems
in Your hands.

Thank You for the Miracle

Dear God,
Thank you for the gift of my son. From the first moment I saw him, I knew he was a miracle. Thank you that I was blessed and chosen by you to be a mommy. Thank you for baby toes, first words and first steps, for birthday parties and new bicycles, for laughter and tears. Thank you for sticky goodnight kisses and whispered bedside prayers (are you still listening, Lord?).

Thank you for dreaming up boys and for letting me be the mother of one. Whatever happens, I'm still so grateful.

When my heart longs to return to those times of innocence and safety and a young mother's dreams, grant me strength for the day and all the challenges it brings. Because you—Great Creator, loving and powerful God—are still at work.

Help me to rest in that today. I trust in you.
Amen.

I Had So Many Dreams for Him

LINDA

After I gave birth to my son Nathan, I thought I'd be able to predict his future. If all went well, he'd roll over, sit up, and babble at the correct ages. When he got older, he would potty at the right time and always look both ways and know how to dial 911. No one on earth could convince me he wasn't the world's most wonderful boy.

Yet somewhere along the journey, my son took a detour. He crawled outside the kid I dreamed he'd become and wandered off. Maybe your son did too, and you don't know how it happened.

Maybe your child has a medical condition, or maybe he's got a drug problem. Maybe he's a rebellious teen, or maybe the doctors just can't figure out what's wrong. Well-meaning people say it's a stage, he'll grow out of it, and maybe he will. But in the meantime, you have two sons: the one you hoped for and the one who stands before you.

If other children tease him or, worse, ignore him, you suffer too. When you think it isn't possible for him to do anything more to shock you, he does. After he gets in trouble at school or runs away from home or goes to jail, you burn with shame.

Yet most of us secretly believe this is not our true son. The son who calls us in the middle of the night or doesn't come home for days is only a cruel imitation of the real thing. Tomorrow, next week, next year, he'll suddenly change, and that little lost boy will find his way back.

The night of my son's high-school prom I was forced to alter my own predictions. Even though the weather service forecasted rain, I knew couples would go to the big dance dressed in slinky formals and those rented tuxedos the boys hate. Seventeen-year-old Nathan had already told me he wouldn't be caught dead in a monkey suit and stiff church shoes. He wasn't going.

That night, as usual, Nathan wore a torn black T-shirt and baggy jeans. His thumbs mashed wildly at the control buttons of his video game.

"Would you please not walk in front of the screen while I kill this monster?" he barked at me.

I stepped aside politely and let myself imagine a different scene: *My son is dressed like a prince. In a shy voice he asks me to help him adjust the maroon cummerbund and straighten the silly bow tie. Instead of a game controller he holds a dainty corsage, plump with pink rosebuds and baby's breath. He bought it for his girl with his own money.*

He promises to get the station wagon back in one piece and he'll treat his date like a lady. No drinking or anything else illegal. Back by curfew? Well, duh. But maybe Mom and Dad can look the other way if he's a few minutes late. Just this once, on such an important occasion. Mentally, I get the camera ready to film history, the way I did when he was a newborn, smiling for the first time.

Smile, Nathan.

Just then he turned from his video game and faced me. I wondered if I'd spoken out loud. I saw the angry words on his shirt, read them as they dripped like blood down the front of it. There was a rip in the fabric, but the message was clear: The son I stood daydreaming of, in tux and stiff black shoes, didn't exist. He never existed. My mind laid the camera down. It would be harder to lay aside all that I had wished for him.

I tried hard not to let my boy see disappointment in my eyes. I knew he was in pain, and I didn't want to add any more weight to his hunched shoulders. I held my own private funeral in order to see more clearly: My son wasn't going to be the one I dreamed he would be. Perhaps he wouldn't "grow out of it"—perhaps it wasn't "just a phase." So instead of hanging on to a myth, I would attempt to bury my imaginary son and embrace the one who lives and breathes.

Laying aside those dreams would be agony. The monster of this game would shatter and destroy and rip my heart in two. The sobs would echo in my empty chest. If he knew, Nathan would surely weep alongside me.

I constructed an imaginary altar on which to sacrifice my fears and grief to God. Then I decided I must do something real, something concrete. I found a flat stone in my garden and set it on the driveway. I wrote things on slips of paper, piled them on the rock. The neighbor lady stood staring as I knelt there, crying softly.

On the cold slab went my dreams: the high grades, the awards, the football scholarship that would make me look like a terrific mom. Even Nathan's high-school prom was laid down, although this dream fought to stay alive.

The papers lay heaped on the rock. I shielded a match with one hand and tried to light the pile. I used a lot of matches before a flame took hold.

The facade I had constructed shrank, slowly at first. In the fire the real Nathan began to emerge. When my version of his life finally melted away, a young man I recognized looked back at me.

So I decided to treasure the things that make him unique—that goofy laugh, those pensive blue eyes. The way he used to drive his math teacher crazy, drawing pictures all over the long division, doodling down the edges of every worksheet. I said a prayer for him and for me.

The wind lifted the blackened flakes of paper. Ashes danced on the driveway. The neighbor lady went into her house, and my son called to me from the window. He wanted me to come inside, to see how he had finally killed the monster. I picked up my little altar and carried it into the house.

No matter what sort of trouble our son faces or how many times he hurts us or shatters our illusions, there's a place in every mom's heart that keeps alive a snapshot of the awesome little boy God made. Maybe it's this vision that gives us the courage to finally lay down our dreams for him so we can embrace the one God is still dreaming.

———

Children in a family are like flowers in a bouquet:
there's always one determined to face in an opposite direction
from the way the arranger desires.

MARCELENE COX

From Hero to Zero

Susan and Richard remember how they used to love attending Jeremy's sports events. And Richard had big dreams for his talented son. But when Jeremy turned fourteen, everything changed. It all started to go downhill. It was one thing to lose the dream of a promising athlete, but they were afraid they would lose their son as well.

Jeremy had always loved sports. Not only that, he was good—really good. Whether it was soccer, baseball, basketball—you name it— Jeremy could do it. He was our rising star. And my husband, Richard, had high hopes for our boy's future. Not only that, but Jeremy had always been our "easy" child. He was cheerful and helpful and fun. His older sister, on the other hand, was moody and strong-willed. As a result, it seemed Katie always got more attention than Jeremy, even if it was mostly negative. This may have been a mistake. Maybe we shortchanged Jeremy. But how do you know what's best at the time? I mean, we'd read lots of parenting books and even took a class at our church. We really tried to do everything right. But it's never as simple as they make it sound in the books.

Throughout grade school and into middle school, Jeremy had lots of friends, enjoyed sports, and received consistently good grades. I loved going to his parent-teacher conferences—so positive compared to his sister's. But then a strange thing happened. Shortly after

Katie started high school, everything changed. Just like the ugly duckling, our daughter suddenly turned into a swan. She was truly transformed—not only in appearance, but also in demeanor, attitude, everything. As a result she finally seemed happy. And my husband and I both let out a giant sigh of relief. It seemed our dream family was finally complete. I think it lasted about a week.

Just before Jeremy turned fourteen, things started to change in another direction. Our first signal came when he began to dress differently. Nothing really strange or shocking but not so much like a jock anymore. And that was okay with me; I've always encouraged my kids to be individuals. But not long after that, we got a call from the middle-school counselor, saying that Jeremy had been caught skipping class. Well, we weren't too pleased but figured it was just a fluke. He and his buddies probably thought it was cool to play hooky. And fortunately they'd been caught. Hopefully we'd nip this thing in the bud.

We punished Jeremy by taking away computer and television privileges for two weeks. But within days I got another call from the school counselor. This time she asked me to come in. When we met, she told me she was concerned for Jeremy. She mentioned that he'd been hanging around with a different group of kids—not his regular sports buddies.

"What's wrong with that?" I asked.

"These kids aren't the best influence," she explained. "And not only that, but Jeremy's grades are all down."

"His grades are down?" I asked in disbelief. "How down?"

"He's got several F's right now."

Suddenly I knew this was getting serious. "What should we do?" I asked her.

Together the counselor and I made a plan to keep Jeremy accountable to both the school and us. We agreed on weekly reports. I was glad that she cared about my son.

After the second week we realized we were getting nowhere fast. Jeremy was still cutting, and his grades hadn't improved. Plus he hated feeling like everyone was watching him. But perhaps the worst blow came when Jeremy announced he wasn't going out for basketball.

"But you love basketball," said his stunned dad. "You're so good at it."

"It's your favorite sport," I reminded him.

"Not anymore." And he stomped up to his bedroom and turned up the awful sounding music he'd started listening to lately.

Amazingly, it was Katie who showed the most patience and compassion at this point. "Just give him time," she assured us. "He's probably just going through a stage or something." Coming from her it was almost believable.

But time didn't help. His grades didn't improve, and he was caught cutting class on a regular basis. We soon learned that his new friends used inhalants (huffing) and smoked pot occasionally. We couldn't believe that our son had actually done these things, but the writing seemed to be on the wall. We confronted Jeremy, and he grew angry, saying his friends didn't do that stuff. But we weren't convinced. So my husband and I scheduled a meeting with the counselor to ask her what she thought we should do. We'd known her for years now and trusted her judgment.

"Take Jeremy out of this school," she suggested. "Get him away from these kids."

Once again we sat down and tried to talk to Jeremy, but he was so defensive. Like a powder keg, he'd blow up over anything. Then he'd question our values and core beliefs, while accusing us of being "bad Christians" and judging his new friends. Always he maintained their innocence in regard to substance abuse. We offered to send him to a counselor, but he refused. Finally, in a desperate move, we did remove him from school, and I began to homeschool him, all the while desperately praying for help and direction. Jeremy made improvements, but I didn't think we could play police-parents indefinitely.

Then one day my husband unexpectedly got a good job offer in another town. Despite the fact we'd just moved into a new home, our concerns for Jeremy motivated us to relocate. Naturally, Katie was devastated, but when we explained how it might be Jeremy's only chance, she reluctantly agreed.

I can't say it's all been smooth sailing since our move. Thankfully, Katie has made new friends and is fitting in well now. Jeremy's back in school and has made one good friend and is actually considering going out for track, but he's still not the same Jeremy we knew.

As we ate burgers at McDonald's one Saturday recently, he told me something that offers a pretty big clue about what happened six months ago. Jeremy explained how a friend back at his old school had severely hurt his feelings. Adam had been one of Jeremy's best friends. Both boys were really good athletes—probably the best in the school. Apparently Adam had picked a fight, and Jeremy refused to engage. Other "friends" sided with Adam and called Jeremy a chicken and other mean names. Jeremy felt hurt and humiliated, and to get back at them, he announced that he wouldn't go out for basketball (he'd always been their high scorer). Then he went out and got himself a new bunch of "friends."

I understand now that Jeremy has a very sensitive spirit, and I want to keep my doors of communication open with him in case something like this ever happens again. I believe that working on our communication (and praying a lot) will be the keys to getting through the remainder of his adolescence. Richard and I still hope that Jeremy will return to sports someday, but we've accepted that this is his decision, not ours. We know we can't force him to live out our dreams. We just hope we can be there to encourage him to pursue his own.

=====

Let your child be the teenager he or she wants to be,
Not the adolescent you were or wish you had been.

Laurence Steinberg

Third Time's a Charm

After two of her boys have lost their way, Andrea is determined to keep her baby, Patrick, on the right track. Patrick is already fifteen and has never been in trouble, but Andrea's overprotective attitudes cause friction in the home. How can she keep Patrick from following in his brothers' footsteps?

Patrick says I treat him like a baby, and maybe I am a bit over-protective with him. After what's happened with his two older brothers—they've both been in and out of prison—I can't allow Patrick to end up that way. He's my last chance as a mom, and I want to do everything I can to help him succeed.

I know parenting doesn't come with an instruction manual, but I wish I'd had better skills when Gil and Rory were small. I made so many mistakes. I didn't realize how my drinking problem and two failed marriages would affect them. By the time Patrick came along, Gil was already doing time for a tragic accident that occurred while he was driving under the influence. A young girl died, and Gil was sent to prison for manslaughter. Gil's brother Rory wasn't much better, and he eventually wound up in jail for drug offenses. I know I was a terrible mother to them both.

When Patrick was a toddler, I hit my own bottom and got treatment for my alcoholism. I was divorced for the third time. Patrick's dad disappeared from our lives and left me alone to raise our son.

This might have been disastrous, but one night I attended a local church revival. At the meeting I accepted Jesus as my personal Savior and felt a great weight lifted from my shoulders. I felt as if God was telling me that he would help me raise Patrick to be a godly man. God would help me stay away from alcohol, and if I tried, I could become a much better parent.

So Patrick and I went to church as often as we could. I was a real "Jesus Freak" and put up Bible verses all over the house—even in the bathroom. I took parenting classes at the community center and attended AA meetings. I got career training and found a well-paying job. Aside from the painful visits to my other sons in jail, things went smoothly until Patrick entered adolescence.

When he began to want to do things without me, I panicked. I was sure he'd get in with a bad crowd if I didn't watch him all the time. Of course the more I smothered him, the more he tried to get away.

He began to get interested in political ideas. He's pretty smart—school's always been easy for him—but his ideas about things such as the legalization of marijuana set me off. "Chill, Mom," he'd say. "Just because I'm reading about pot doesn't mean I'm smoking it." Since there was no other evidence that he was involved with drugs, I let it go, but I began to give all his friends the third degree when he brought them home.

"What church do you go to?" was one of the first things I'd ask if Pat brought a buddy over. Then I'd eyeball the kid, judging him by his haircut or what his T-shirt said. If I suspected the boy listened to the "wrong" music or might be a bad influence, I'd tell Pat he needed a new friend. Pat stopped bringing his friends home and started making excuses to get out of family activities. He holed up in his room for hours on end and spoke to me only when necessary.

One evening I knocked on his bedroom door, and he didn't answer right away. I thought, *This is it; he's probably in there shooting dope.* I crashed into his room and found him sitting on his bed, sorting baseball cards.

Patrick stared at me. "I know you don't trust me," he said, "but I'm not like my brothers. I just need a chance to be me."

I shook my head. "I'm trying to help you turn out better than your brothers. I don't want you to make bad choices the way they have. Don't you see, baby? You're my last hope."

Patrick looked like he might cry, but then he shoved all his baseball cards to the floor. "I'm not a baby anymore!" he shouted. "I can think for myself! Get out!" My feelings were so hurt; my heart felt scraped raw.

I felt so alone—like both God and Patrick had abandoned me. It took everything I had to keep from falling off the wagon. I got out my Bible and tried to pray. I read the proverb about training up a child in the way he should go and asked myself if I had done that with Patrick. *Yes,* I thought, *I really have done my best.* "When he is old he will not turn from it," the scripture said. And then it was like a light bulb came on. I had been thinking all this was about me when it was really about Patrick. I'd given him the training and knew he had a ways to go before he was fully grown. But by being paranoid that he'd become as lost as Gil and Rory, I wasn't giving him a chance at all. I needed to stop smothering him and let him grow up.

I apologized to my son and started working on loosening my grip a little. I still keep a sharp eye out for signs of trouble—it would be hard for anything to get past me—but I'm trying to respect Patrick's choices and pick my battles. Pat's a great kid. With a lot of God's help and maybe a little less of mine, I pray he'll grow up to be a godly man.

───

If there is anything that we wish to change in our children,
we should first examine it and see whether it is not something
that could better be changed in ourselves.

CARL G. JUNG

It's a Boy

When Evelyn learned that her son had gotten his girlfriend pregnant, she imagined her world and her son's hopes for the future were over. She pushed John and his girlfriend, Michelle, to have an abortion. She wept and pleaded. Who could have guessed that someday she'd be overwhelmingly grateful for losing such an important battle?

I remember it was Halloween night when my son John and his girlfriend, Michelle, broke the news. At first I thought they were joking.

"Pregnant?" I asked. "Are you kidding?"

They assured me that they weren't, but even more disconcerting, they didn't seem upset or even fazed. Michelle, dressed in black cat ears and a long black tail attached to her behind, appeared even happy.

When I was finally convinced that they were telling the truth, I began to cry. Then I began to get angry. I pummeled my son with questions. How could he have let this happen, especially now? How could they have been so stupid and careless? How could this happen when they were supposed to both be strong Christians who didn't do that kind of thing? (At the time I didn't know God personally myself.)

To make matters worse, in recent months John had been receiving offers to attend college on a full basketball scholarship. On top of that he was the senior class president, and I was the chair of the senior party. He was my bright and shining star, a huge relief after his older brother's lackluster high-school career. Since my husband, John Sr., had died five years before, John had been my "little man."

Still sitting at the dining room table, I swiped at my tears and running mascara. Nothing would ever be the same. My son's life was over!

Then suddenly a huge wave of relief washed over me. *Of course! Michelle would simply have to have an abortion.* I would happily pay for it. Maybe no one would even have to know about this!

"Surely," I said to them, "you're not intending to have this baby."

Yes, they told me: They were having this baby. What's more, they were getting married over Christmas break. They'd already talked it through with each other and with a teacher at school. It was all decided.

I felt like someone had slammed a two-by-four into my chest. "You've got to be kidding," I said again. But I could see that they weren't. I spent the next two hours pleading with them to abort this baby. But rather than see reason, Michelle blindly refused the idea, even implying that I was horrible, some kind of murderer, to consider such a thing.

I don't know how I made it through the next few months, but I did. I had no choice. I helped plan the wedding, a stone in my gut. I withdrew from chairing the senior party. The colleges that had been courting John withdrew their offers. Seeing no other way, I helped John find a job where he could work part-time and then move into full time after the school year ended.

Following their December wedding, John and Michelle got an

apartment and started married life. I didn't see them much. I couldn't bear to watch Michelle's belly grow with what I viewed as a wrecking ball to my son's life.

On the morning the baby was born, I got a phone call from John. "Your first grandson was just born, Mom."

My first grandson? Yes, of course. It was.

I got in my car and began the half-hour drive to the hospital. Almost immediately, for reasons I couldn't understand, I began to cry. I cried all the way there. By the time I reached the maternity ward, I was a blubbering mess.

John met me with a huge bear hug. He didn't ask why I was crying. Then he handed over the bundle that was Jonathan Carter III. The baby's tiny fist gripped my finger, and a small bubble rested on his lower lip. I felt as if my heart would fall out, it was so heavy with love.

I instantly adored Jonathan and still do. You've never seen a more dedicated, loving grandmother than me! Today he is seven years old. He's a beautiful treasure with blond hair, bright blue eyes, long skinny legs, and, for better or worse, my nose.

Sometimes I am overcome with guilt about wanting to abort Jonathan. What if my son and daughter-in-law had listened to me?

John and Michelle, against all odds and in spite of several rocky years, are still together. Once a month or so I attend church with them. I am understanding more and more about God and being a Christian and what it really means.

These days John is going to college part time and plans to teach high school—and, not surprisingly, be a coach as well. He wants to make a difference in kids' lives, he says. And I know he will.

Another Sleepless Night

MELODY

When you were tiny and helpless
You woke me with cries of hunger
Now you wake me with your cries of silence
Your bed is not slept in tonight
Your room is dark and cold and empty
How is your heart?

If I could, I would make you come home
Right this instant
And I would tell you that I love you
And that everything's going to be okay
But is it?

You want to be in charge of your life now
All grown up
And yet you still reason like a child
It's hard to have one foot in each world
How long must you linger there?
How long can I endure this night?

Yet with only faith to hold me,
I will believe for the day
When you will finally realize

Your value, your worth
Not just to me, but to yourself
And to God
How long will it take?

Keeper of Hopes and Dreams

Dear Lord,
  When my son arrived in the world, every dream seemed possible. I thought those dreams were from you. But now I'm not so sure. Did I just make up those expectations out of youthful inexperience and silly pride?

I know you remember every dream my son had growing up. He wanted so many lives—truck driver, conductor, Mafia hit man, space warrior, baseball legend, rock star. Sometimes he just wanted to make one perfect sandcastle, to have one day with no pimples, to meet one pretty girl who would say yes.

Please care for his best dreams today, the ones that bring him closer to your good will for his life. And show me what dreams for him I should put away now. Breathe into my heart today the new dreams for my son that are from you.

Amen.

Section Three

HOW DID WE END UP HERE?

MELODY

I f you're like me, you've spent a fair amount of time trying to make sense of your son's life. You go over various pieces of his childhood, trying to figure out exactly what happened. You ask yourself when and where he first got off track. Maybe we think that if we can pinpoint a certain event, we might be able to fix everything. Because that's what we moms do, isn't it? We fix things. With a Band-Aid and a kiss, we can make everything okay.

I always knew there was something unique about my firstborn. I'd majored in early childhood education, and I knew that each child was different. But something about Gabe's intensity as a baby always got everyone's attention. Some called him difficult, some thought he was spoiled, but I just thought he was my precious blue-eyed darling. He was an intense preschooler too, needy and clingy, but filled with a delightful curiosity and a probing intelligence. He learned to read by age four, did simple math shortly thereafter, and was kicked out of kindergarten because he was "just not emotionally ready." I sadly took him home and figured *they* simply weren't ready for *him*.

In grade school he was immediately identified as highly gifted and for the first several years received some special attention for this. But at the same time, his troubles began popping up like weeds. Soon I was "doing time" at his school, either helping in the classroom or dealing with his latest discipline problem—irritating behaviors like disrupting class, squabbling with peers, spitting, writing on a desk. You name it; by fourth grade Gabe had probably done it. Some teachers were compassionate, saying things like "Gabe's not a bad boy; he just does things his way" or "He hears a different drummer." You know, the sorts of things you may have heard too. Words meant to take away the sting of embarrassment.

So like many parents with a "difficult child," we looked for ways to make things better. We tried sports, Scouts, swim team, art lessons, church activities, homeschool, private school—anything to help our son get beyond this…this…whatever it was! And while we'd have brief moments of hope, Gabe continued to be a square peg in a round hole, and his discipline problems increased. On top of all this, he began to grow painfully shy, but not too shy to act out. After a psychological evaluation, the term ADD (a new diagnosis at the time) began to attach itself, but by then Gabe was just entering adolescence, and our doctor's concern over teen hormones and experimental medications made us decide not to try drug therapy.

In middle school things seemed to improve—fewer calls from school, better grades. We thought maybe he was outgrowing "this thing." And yet our son didn't quite fit in, didn't socialize with peers, and barely spoke to us. He was an extreme loner. As he reached his late teens, his isolation increased. Still we thought maybe this was just his personality: a book person, a computer whiz, an intelligent eccentric. And besides, his SAT scores were the highest in the school (although his GPA was in the toilet). Never did we dream "this thing" was something more serious. After all, how do you know what's "normal" in an adolescent? How can you tell what's cause for concern?

In his second year of college, Gabe turned twenty, and a time bomb exploded inside his brain. He experienced a full-blown psychotic episode, nonstop, for an entire month. He saw monstrous things, heard evil voices, smelled nonexistent odors, and believed that his life was in serious danger. Living away from home at the time, he attempted to "deal with it" by draping his windows with layers of blankets, barricading himself with furniture, disabling his computer, and literally starving himself (he suspected he was being poisoned). Finally, at the end of his strength, he called home and said, "Mom, I think I'm losing my mind."

When I went to pick him up, we talked at length, and he confessed to having experimented with various hallucinogenic drugs in the previous months. He said that at first he thought he was simply experiencing the aftereffects of those mind-bending chemicals. But weeks after he discontinued the use of the drugs, his symptoms hadn't gone away. And since he'd taken a lot of psychology classes (including abnormal psychology), he felt certain something was seriously wrong with him.

My firstborn's diagnosis of schizophrenia was the hardest thing I've ever had to walk through. And for a short while I feared that we had lost him—or could lose him—permanently. During that dark time, it was only prayer and the grace of God that kept me going. Thankfully, Gabe received excellent treatment and amazing new meds, and now, two years later, he is honestly functioning better than ever before.

Of course, our story's not yet over. Whose story ever is? But incredibly, as I studied the symptoms of this insidious illness, all those things from his childhood suddenly made sense. All those puzzling pieces began to fit together. At last I began to understand what we'd been dealing with. We finally had an explanation. And although it was a painful one, it was accompanied by a small portion of comfort—and hope.

How did we end up here? Why did God give us sons with serious problems and challenges to face? Maybe we'll never know for sure. Or maybe there's a hidden blessing in there somewhere. Perhaps one day it'll all make perfect sense. But in the meantime, we get to trust that God knows what he's doing in our sons' lives—and we get to love them and continue to hope for the best. Isn't that what we mothers do?

Love...
bears all things,
believes all things,
hopes all things,
endures all things.
Love never fails.

1 CORINTHIANS 13:4,7-8

Home Is Where
the Safe Is

When Trudy Hanson first suspected that her boys, Evan, sixteen, and Erik, fourteen, had been stealing cash and other valuables at home, she and her husband, Rick, didn't want to believe it. But when they discovered twenty dollars missing from Trudy's purse, the Hansons knew they had a problem.

The first time it happened I'd made some extra money watching the neighbor's baby and treated myself to a haircut. After the hairdresser finished, I opened my wallet to pay her. I was sure I'd stashed the money in a side pocket. But the pocket was empty, and my haircut money was nowhere to be found.

I thought I'd either misplaced the cash or else my husband had had an emergency and had taken it to work. But when I asked him about it, he said he hadn't touched the money. I couldn't stand the thought of accusing Evan or Erik of stealing from me. So I just assumed I'd lost it somewhere.

I grew up in a small Midwestern farming community where people left their houses unlocked and theft was rare. When we moved to a large city on the East Coast last year, we had a lot of things to adjust to—but I didn't think stealing would be one of them. Respecting the property of others is very important to me. I've always taught our boys this principle. The family rule has always been "Don't touch things that aren't yours without asking."

Our boys had made the move as smoothly as we could expect, but it wasn't long before they each brought home new friends who were much different from those they'd had in the Midwest. These new buddies were streetwise and a lot more hard edged. A few months after we arrived, one of my sons' acquaintances was arrested for joyriding—stealing a car and abandoning it in a field. A short while later another boy Evan knew from school was busted for dealing crack cocaine. I was still convinced our kids wouldn't get into those things, but Rick and I demanded that our sons find some new friends.

I put the haircut incident behind me, still believing I'd carelessly lost the money. But when Rick noticed several of his compact discs and videotapes missing from the entertainment center, our suspicions were again aroused. We confronted Evan, who denied he had taken them. Erik said, "Why would I want your old-fogy music? Give me a break."

The only other possibility was that we'd been burglarized. But why would a burglar take inexpensive items and leave more expensive things such as jewelry and electronic equipment? Nothing added up.

For the next year small items and amounts of cash disappeared at odd times. After a painful root canal, Rick's pain medication went missing. An heirloom ring with a small diamond vanished from my jewelry box. Each time our boys denied their involvement.

Then one night I went to my bedroom to get the reading glasses I'd left in my purse. I was shocked to see Erik standing there with my wallet in his hands. "What do you think you're doing?" I nearly shouted, and he mumbled something about needing to know my driver's license number.

Rick heard the commotion and confronted Erik, demanding that he remove his shoes. My son took off his sneakers, and a twenty-dollar bill fluttered to the floor. He turned red, and I burst into tears. Erik explained how he'd gotten himself into trouble by borrowing money from one of his new streetwise pals. When he couldn't repay the loan on time, Erik claimed he'd been threatened. "I was afraid to ask for help," he said. And then he admitted that the loan was to purchase marijuana.

Erik entered a drug treatment program, uncooperatively at first. After several months of intensive counseling and strictly enforced house rules, he apologized for stealing from us. Later we discovered that Evan was guilty, too, and that both of them had taken things when they needed money. Evan left home for six months rather than stop using drugs.

We learned how naive we were—the movies and compact discs had been taken to used-record shops for cash, and my sons had pawned my great aunt's ring. I was furious and locked my feelings away, refusing to speak to either of them except when necessary.

In order to feel secure we installed a safe in which to keep valuables and my purse. We locked our doors at all times. I felt guilty and ashamed for failing to teach Erik and Evan the importance of honesty and for leaving small-town life in the Midwest.

I'll admit that for a long time I was angry with God as well as the boys. I'd tried so hard to raise them to be honest and upright. I'd done everything I knew to instill good character. To have my own flesh and blood steal from me felt like a huge violation, and I thought it implied that I was a bad parent too. Over and over I asked God, "How did we end up like this?" I wondered if I could ever trust my sons again.

Gradually I grew into the idea that perhaps forgiveness was the key. If I could not forgive my sons for their mistakes, they might never change. And if I didn't forgive myself for my shortcomings as a mother, I might never stop being mad about our circumstances.

Bit by bit I've forgiven my sons for the hurt they've caused, and little by little my sons have changed for the better. To keep Evan and Erik from being tempted again, the safe still guards my possessions. But I no longer give my boys the silent treatment. Locking Evan and Erik out of my heart is something I'll never be able to do.

Yell Point

LINDA

Teddy Roosevelt's famous advice to "speak softly and carry a big stick" was probably intended for me and any mom like me. We know who we are. We're the yellers, those mothers who can crank up the decibels above any stereo, moms who can call a late child in from a mile away.

I won't say how much I've screamed at my offspring over the years, but my boys dubbed me "Old Yeller," if that's any indication. I frequently read them the riot act, and it got louder as they got older. By the time they were in their teens, you'd think I'd have become permanently hoarse, but unfortunately my lungs had matured along with their hormones.

Even though I have been a yeller all my mothering years (I began having yelling contests with my boys when they were toddlers), I wasn't always this way, and I don't really believe in it. In fact, I grew up in a family where yelling was considered poor form. Which, of course, it is. And worse than being poor form, I know that it's hardly effective. It doesn't solve anything. Teachers, psychologists, and even your nosy neighbor will tell you that raising your voice to a child only makes him tune you out.

So why do we mothers of lost boys so often resort to screaming?

I think we do it in part because we don't know what else to do.

How do you ground a kid who never leaves his room anyway? You can't take away his car if it's been impounded. Time-outs seem sort of silly by now. And forcing an almost-grown man to sit on a stool facing the corner just doesn't fly, especially when he turns it into a laughing and belching fest. (Believe it or not, I tried this once.)

I think another reason we yell is that screaming is the ultimate illusion of power. It's a way to vent and release our own emotions while we imagine that it makes us more heard. The first part is true. The second part couldn't be further from the truth.

If you have a troubled teenage son and you struggle with yelling, you probably have a friend or two who can relate, which is comforting. She understands why you sound so hoarse. She's probably been dishing out her own speeches all day: "How many times have I told you…" followed by "You got *what* pierced?" and "If you come home one more time reeking of beer…" Most of those talks were punctuated by her offspring's denial and fueled by an escalation of mutual anger.

But yelling probably is not something you and your friend are proud of. And it's probably not something you discuss the way you talk about dieting or working out. "I've just got to quit screaming like a banshee at these kids" isn't quite the same as moaning about the size of your thighs or vowing to get to the gym three times a week. Cellulite and a hot temper don't go hand in hand, although there doesn't seem to be much anyone can do about either problem.

Or is there?

I'm asking God to help me figure out exactly where my "yell point" is—the moment when I go over the edge of that controlled monotone teachers use and the spot where I begin to cascade down a mountain of madness, blasting my kids with all the lung power I can muster.

You probably have a yell point too. If you and I can learn what sorts of things put us over the edge and transform us from Dear Mom to Old Yeller, we may be able to save our yells for the times that really matter. Then we'll at least have some hope that our boys won't grow up to become yelling men. (That picture stops me cold.)

I want to learn how to be a better listener and communicate with my boys without the booming voice. I'm going to work on it hard. The big stick...well, I'm still thinking about that.

A Fishy Story

Gloria and her husband, John, have one son, Forrest, and a baby daughter, Jessica. Forrest had always been a good kid, and Gloria credited a lot of that to his constant attendance at church youth group meetings and his close walk with God. Gloria and John often wondered why other families were so lenient, didn't make their kids go to church, and gave them too much rope. Then, one day, their conviction that their son was on the right path was challenged.

Forrest has always been active, upbeat, talkative. And he's also always been a strong Christian. His youth group meant the world to him. He never missed a meeting, and even through his early teen years I didn't worry much about his getting into trouble. If he came home late, that was okay. He was usually out with other Christian kids from church.

I often wondered why other Christian parents weren't more careful with their kids or didn't require them to be in church. One day I got a call from one of my friends who had a lot of trouble with her boys. Stacey sounded especially strung out and worried. I waited for the bomb to drop, assuming one of her kids had done something worse than usual. *Remember not to be judgmental,* I told myself.

But instead of relating her latest teen crisis, she said something that totally confused me. "I'm so sorry about Forrest, Gloria."

"Sorry about what?" I asked. "He's doing great."

"You mean you don't know?" I heard sincere surprise in Stacey's voice.

"Don't know what? What are you talking about?" I demanded.

"Oh, Gloria. I don't think I should be the one...I just assumed..."

"Okay," I said, "now you're freaking me out. What on earth did Forrest do?"

"Well...," Stacey said. "Actually, you see... Gosh I hate being the one... Forrest was on the front page of our town's little newspaper today. It says he and a friend were both arrested last Thursday for robbing the local fly-fishing shop."

I was too stunned to speak but quickly calculated that, yes, Forrest had been in her area then. I asked her to read the article to me. It was hard to hear because I was in shock, but even worse, the story was actually *funny.*

Forrest and his friend had entered the shop first thing in the morning. One boy, the article explained, took the shop's owner out back and asked him to demonstrate a rod for him. The other one proceeded to grab all he could—an expensive yellow fishing jacket, numerous rods, boots, etc.—and put them in the car. Before the boys left, they asked the owner where the best places to fly-fish were. He gave them directions to the best spot in the area.

As soon as the boys were gone, the owner noticed one lone boot of a pair. A quick inventory revealed he'd been robbed, and he called the police. The authorities found the culprits within twenty minutes. You can guess where. Forrest and his friend were happily fishing the area's best spot, the one the owner had directed them to. They were using their new equipment, one of them sporting a new yellow jacket.

When Stacey finished the article, I was too stunned to speak. I had to hang up so I could cry and call my husband. When John and I finally had Forrest in front of us and confronted him, his story relieved us some. He swore up and down that he'd had no idea what his friend was up to or had done until they got to the fishing hole.

As we waited for his court date, I agonized for Forrest, who had just turned eighteen. The other kid was only seventeen, so he wouldn't be in danger of facing the same kinds of consequences Forrest would. And it was all the younger kid's fault! We decided Forrest's best bet was to plead guilty with a full explanation. I went with him and told the judge what a good boy Forrest really was. I reminded him that it was this other boy who actually took the stuff from the store. I begged him not to give Forrest any jail time.

When he ordered Forrest to two days in jail, I was absolutely furious. I broke down crying. I just couldn't handle the idea of my son in jail.

As the day approached, I was tormented. I imagined the strip search and checking of orifices routinely performed on check-in at a jail. Then I found out that he'd spend his first twenty-four hours in "lock up." He'd be in a dark room alone, with no food and nothing to do but think. I worried and worried about what this would do to Forrest emotionally. And I prayed.

When Forrest came out of jail two days later, he confessed that contrary to what I'd believed, he'd been in on the crime plan all along.

And he'd been dabbling in dope and drinking for quite some time. His relationship with God was not what it had been. Now he wanted to come clean, start fresh.

"I'll never be the same, Mom," he told me. "Jail was the best thing that could have happened to me."

Needless to say, I learned a lot of valuable, painful lessons from the ordeal. Never again will I judge any mother who is trying her best but has kids who are in trouble. Nor will I falsely assume that "good" kids can't do bad things.

It's been two years now since that incident. Forrest is, as far as I can tell, walking closely with God. He moved to Colorado a year ago and attends church there while he works full time at, believe it or not, a fly-fishing shop.

———

The wildest colts make the best horses.

THEMISTOCLES

Happy Mother's Day

Rosa's son Juan had been in and out of trouble since high school. Yet she and her husband had been supportive of him, gotten him counseling, encouraged him to graduate through the flex school program, and finally had begun to hope that these problems were behind them now. But when Rosa learned that Juan had spent Mother's Day in jail, she was devastated.

Juan's definitely been our wild child. He's the youngest of our three children and perhaps a little spoiled, but he's a likable kid. We always hoped he'd outgrow his troubles.

I'm not entirely sure why, but during his teen years Juan had little respect for the law or even policemen. It's not like he was some hardened criminal, but he never seemed to care about what people thought of him. He thought laws were stupid and most rules were just waiting to be broken. Surprisingly, he never got into any serious trouble. But he did get into trouble. And to be honest, it all seemed pretty serious at the time—at least to me.

His first run-in with the law seems silly now, but at the time my husband and I were really upset. Juan and a friend were arrested for stealing pop from the local deli. Both boys had money to pay but decided they didn't want to wait in line. Since it was their first offense, they simply appeared before a jury of their peers and were sentenced to community service and probation. In time their records were expunged. The whole thing was so humiliating (for me), and I hoped my son got the message that crime does not pay!

Juan's next offense came about a year later in the form of an "MIP" (minor in possession of alcohol), and this would go on his permanent record. Fortunately, since his earlier offense had been expunged, this appeared as his first criminal offense, and he got off with a small fine, lecture, and judicial slap on the wrist. Perhaps the most shocking thing to me that day was how full the courtroom was with boys who were in trouble for the same thing—or worse. And yet it was still a humiliating experience for me.

Juan seemed sorry and worked hard to pay his fine. But he still hung out with a wild group of friends—not a gang exactly, but they were kids who weren't afraid of trouble or the law. Juan sometimes missed his curfew, but he was eighteen now. At this stage we just wanted him to get his high-school diploma. To continually fight over curfew seemed like a lose-lose situation to us. Plus we found that the less we pushed Juan, the more he obeyed our rules.

Juan had worked hard to save enough money to buy his first car. It was pretty bad, but it ran—most of the time. However, we weren't too comfortable at the thought of him behind the wheel on a rainy night, especially if he were impaired in any way. And despite his reassurances that he would never drive under the influence, we could never be sure.

One spring night Juan came home on foot.

"Where's your car?" I asked.

"It's a piece of junk," he said.

"Yeah, I know," I answered, "but what happened to it?"

He then told me it had broken down on the side of the road a couple of miles from home. My husband drove by to make sure it wasn't a safety hazard, then returned home. "We'll tow it back in the morning," he told my son.

But the next day Juan's car was gone. We couldn't figure it out, and to be perfectly honest, my husband and I hoped it was gone for good. But we reported the car stolen. Juan asked around town, and a story slowly emerged. It seems Juan's "friends" had heard him complaining about his "piece of junk" the night before (after it had broken down for the umpteenth time), and one of the guys asked him what he was going to do to it. Juan had flippantly said, "Oh, I just wish someone would blow the stupid thing up." Well, as it turned out, that's exactly what his friends did.

"Nice friends," I said.

"They're not really my friends, Mom," said Juan. "Just some guys I know."

Still, his car was gone now, and along with it the fear of a bad accident. My husband and I felt relieved, and we encouraged Juan to use his bike to get around. And so he did, and life seemed to slow down a bit for all of us.

Then on Mother's Day weekend, my husband and I wanted to go visit my mom. I wanted Juan to come too, but he had to work. I was terribly disappointed because Mother's Day is a big deal in my family. But my husband didn't think Juan should risk his job. So I looked my son in the eyes and made him promise that he'd stay out of trouble while we were gone. "I promise, Mom," he said. "Just consider it your Mother's Day present from me. And don't worry."

But I started to worry on Saturday night when I called home and no one answered. I figured he was just out with friends, hopefully keeping his promise and not getting into trouble. But when he still didn't answer the phone on Sunday, I grew more concerned. Maybe it was mother's intuition, but I remember praying specifically that God would do something to get my boy's attention before he got into some really big trouble.

We got home around five o'clock, and there was no sign of Juan. I called his best friend to discover that my son was in jail. He'd been arrested the night before.

As it turned out, Juan was in jail because his so-called friends (the ones who'd torched his car) had dumped the remains in a national forest—a pretty serious crime actually. But because the car belonged to Juan, he was charged, arrested, and jailed until someone (like a parent) came home and posted bail.

Well, Happy Mother's Day to me, I thought, as we headed for the county jail. Fortunately, we were able to bail him out that night. And after that, Juan had to work hard within the judicial system to get the whole thing cleared up. But during that time, he really got to see, up close and personal, how "the system" works (and sometimes doesn't). I think this might've finally taught him to respect the law (or at least what the law can do when you break it or are accused of breaking it).

Now I think that having my son thrown in jail was really the best Mother's Day gift of all. I think Juan learned a lesson that weekend, and thankfully, he hasn't been in trouble with the law again.

My Son, My Son, Why Have You Forsaken Me?

MELODY

For nine months I carried you in my body,
Stretching to the limits to contain you.
Body and soul,
We were one, you and I,
In perfect harmony.

Oh, the agony of birthing!
But instantly I forgave my pain
When I became lost in your placid blue eyes.
And I gave you my heart
To do with as you pleased.

I fed you from my very breast,
Whispering I love you.
Even in the middle of the night,
I always heard your cries.
And I came quickly.

I watched you grow before my eyes.
I ran beside you on your new bike.
And I bandaged your cuts,

Nursed you while you had the measles.
Nothing I wouldn't do for my little man.

I watched teary-eyed as you stood outside
Waiting for that big yellow bus
To swallow you up
And take you away from me.
But there were cookies when you came home.

Then came soccer balls, baseballs, hamsters, and lizards.
Sports and Scouts and wide toothy smiles.
Long legs and smelly tennis shoes.
Magic tricks and practical jokes
That made me laugh!

Quickly, you grew—taller, older, more handsome.
Independent, surly, and a little withdrawn.
Unsure of yourself, yet cocky;
Questioning, rebelling, sometimes yelling.
But I still loved you.

Harder and harder now you push against me,
My values, my morals, my teachings.
Saying that none of these are your own
And that you do not need me.
You slam your door in my face!

My son, my son, why have you forsaken me?

What can I do but pray?
Night after night, with tears,

I pray that God will keep you safe.
Your body, your mind, your spirit.
And all I can do is believe.

I raised you the best I could,
Teaching what I thought you should know.
And perhaps the day will come
When you will realize this
And return to me
And to the One who made you.

What Were You Thinking?

L ord,
You gave me the gift of a son, but some days your gift makes me despair. He's walking proof that I failed at my most important job in life. You created me to be a mother—and to expect the joyful rewards of a family. And now this.

Why did you make raising a son so difficult? Why did you make a mother's heart so ready to give all, hope all, believe all...and yet so ready to break? Why couldn't you make love safe?

Lord, I need to be a source of nurture and encouragement, of wisdom and grace, but I'm feeling weak and afraid. And I don't want to break anymore.

Help me. Be strength for me. Be a refuge for my family. Be a net of safety under us. And if my heart should break again, make all the pieces beautiful for your purposes, especially for my son.

Amen.

Part II

WHAT IS...

I FEAR FOR HIS
SAFETY, HIS SOUL

MELODY

For me, one of the toughest challenges in raising my sons has been the fear that they will get seriously hurt—either physically or spiritually. Maybe you know what I mean. Maybe you've experienced that gripping fear that seizes upon you when you wake up in the middle of the night and realize that your son has missed his curfew—perhaps by several hours. Your heart begins to race as you pace the floor, trying not to imagine the worst. And if you're like me, you pray. You pray real hard. Just over a year ago I went through three days plagued with the fear that I'd lost my younger son—for good. Even now it seems like yesterday...

It's early spring, warmer than usual with promises of a good summer ahead. Luke is nineteen and, we hope, beyond some of the troubles of his youth. We know now that he's struggled with drug abuse for a couple of years. It's been an off-and-on thing. He stays clean and free and responsible for months at a time, and then suddenly, for no apparent reason, he takes the plunge again, going down...down...down... But it's been quite some time now, and we're feeling positive. He's been working with his dad lately and doing a good job too. We feel hopeful. We think we might be out of the woods.

But not quite. It's Friday, and Luke decides to ride his bike into town to visit some friends, he says. Well, this always makes us a little uncomfortable because we know there are "some friends" in town who aren't always the best influence. But we've had lots of talks with Luke in the past couple of months, and he always reassures us that he can stand up to the pressure; he's his own man now, clean and sober, and we shouldn't worry so much. And besides that, we realize that it's his life and these are his choices. Other than drawing some firm lines and loving him unconditionally, there's little else we can do. Well, other than praying, of course. And believe me, we do a lot of that.

I try not to get too worried when Luke doesn't return that evening. I tell myself he's nineteen, old enough to be on his own now. He's probably just sleeping over somewhere, I reason, because despite the sunny day, the temperature here in the mountains still drops down to twenty at night. And then I go to bed and pray myself to sleep. I pray for my son's safety; I pray for his soul.

I arise early the next morning, put on a pot of coffee, and tiptoe out to where my two sons live in the guesthouse (just twenty feet from our house). Luke has not come home. I pray some more and try to distract myself with writing and puttering about, but I nervously glance out the window each time I see a car or pedestrian pass. And I pray again for Luke's safety because I have this gut feeling (call it mother's instinct) that all is not well with my younger son.

I make a couple of phone calls. "Haven't seen him..." is all I get for my efforts. But one good friend, Luke's best friend, sounds concerned too. So I hop in my car and drive into town. I search all of Luke's regular haunts. Not here, not there, no one has seen him. And my heart begins to pound with that panicky feeling as I wonder where he could be. What could he be doing?

Evening comes, and now my husband is worried too. He goes out to Luke's room to do a "check." We've told Luke many times that as long as he lives at home, we maintain the right to do a room check anytime we have an honest cause to suspect that he's using drugs or alcohol. My husband returns with evidence: used hypodermic needles, a candle stub, a gritty spoon. Luke hasn't even bothered to hide them; perhaps it's a cry for help, my husband says.

My eyes blur as I stare down at the bright orange plungers of the syringes. We've seen these things before. But it's been a while, and that last time, several months ago, we'd hoped we'd never see them again. And here they are, back again, stark and cruel, mocking me from my kitchen counter. Now fear rises in me like a fever, and I swallow back my tears. "What can we do?" I ask. And my husband just shakes his head and goes to the other room.

I know perfectly well what we can do. It's what we always do. We can wait. And, of course, we can pray. But it's the waiting that gets to you. Especially when you've been "blessed" with an active imagination. Suddenly images of Luke assault me—his body lifeless and pale in a frozen ditch somewhere or unconscious in the backseat of some old car. Where is he? Where is my son? Can you see him, God?

By the third day, I feel partially dead inside. It's as if I'm grieving, as if my younger son has actually died. I tell myself I'm being ridiculous, that Luke's probably just fine, but I don't believe a word I say.

I drive through town again, stopping at a store where a "friend" of his works. She's not a bad person, but I know she's involved in the drug community. I wait near the counter until no one's nearby, and then I tell her who I am and that I'm worried about Luke. I feel stupid, afraid she'll laugh or think I'm neurotic, overprotective, perhaps even remind me that Luke's nineteen now, not a kid anymore. But she surprises me with her concerned eyes. She's a mother too, she tells me, and Luke's a good boy, really. Then she says she'll make some phone calls and get back to me. I want to hug her. But instead I say thanks and self-consciously back away. I go home and wait by the phone.

She calls and says she's located him. I ask where. She says she can't say, that it would get her in trouble. And then I realize it's serious—it's drugs. But she's told him to call me. And he has promised he will. So I wait and wait, relieved to know he's alive, yet worried just the same.

Several hours later he calls. He tells me he's fine, and I begin to cry. "Don't you know how worried we've been?" I say. "It's been three days. Three long, horrible days! You could've been dead." He actually laughs but not with real humor. Then he promises to explain everything when he gets home.

"When will that be?" I ask.

"Tonight," he promises, then hangs up.

His dad and I decide it's time for action, intervention, something. We decide on an ultimatum: Luke can either get professional treatment or move out. We make some preliminary calls and find out a bed is free in a detox clinic in a neighboring town. We're all ready to do this but decide to call our Christian psychologist friend first.

"Yes, that's a sensible plan," he agrees. Then he adds, "Make sure you pray about it though. God could direct you differently." And so we pray about it again.

When Luke gets home, we're prepared for resistance, denial, arguments, even tantrums. We've seen it all. But Luke surprises us. He agrees. He knows he needs help, perhaps even detox. But he says something in him has changed for good this time. And then he goes into a long, detailed story of the last three days. Of how he went to tell his drug connections that he was done, finished, and not to call him anymore. But because he owed them money (of course, they couldn't let him go that easily!), they "detained" him. And essentially, Luke got to endure his own three long, horrible days in the "belly of the whale." And he got to see his "friends" in a whole new light—for what and who they really are. And he didn't like it much. And he assures us it's really over now. Then to prove it, he spends the following two weeks at home—detoxing himself and passing random drug tests. I send flowers to his friend at the store—to thank her.

Are we out of the woods yet? It looks good, but who knows? I still experience that gut-wrenching fear occasionally. I'm a mother, after all. Isn't panic part of our job description? But it's that kind of fear that can drive us to our knees. It's a reminder that in many ways we are powerless over our sons' choices. But we can still pray. We can come before the One with real power—the One who loves the lost— and we can ask him to keep our boys safe, both in body and soul.

But let all those rejoice who put their trust in You;
Let them ever shout for joy, because You defend them;
Let those also who love Your name
Be joyful in You.

PSALM 5:11

I Wasn't Prepared for a Prodigal

GIGI GRAHAM TCHIVIDJIAN

Gigi Graham Tchividjian, popular author and speaker, is the daughter of world-renowned evangelist Billy Graham. When one of her sons began to drift away from God and his family, she was stunned. She hadn't expected problems like this. After all, she and her husband had tried their hardest to raise their kids in a godly way. Nothing was "wrong" with the other children. What was going on with her son Tullian?

I stood in the doorway, watching my son walk slowly down the driveway and out into the street. Then, with a heart that felt heavy as lead, I reluctantly turned away.

I forced myself to go through the motions of fixing dinner and doing the evening chores. When I finally crawled into bed, I lay awake, crying and wondering. Where was he? Had he eaten supper? Did he have a place to sleep? Could we have done things differently? Would he ever come home again?

I thought back over the past months. The ups and downs, the emotions, the harsh words, the frustrations, the disobedience, the dishonesty, the questions, the long nights...sitting and waiting, wondering, worrying, asking why.

Why was this son choosing to rebel against all we'd offered him?

A warm, loving home, physical comfort, an education, a godly heritage. We had wanted him, prayed for him, and had been overjoyed at his arrival. He had been such a fun-loving, happy child. We called him our "sunshine."

I never expected to be awakened late at night by police officers holding large dogs on tight leashes at the front door, calls from detention centers, unsavory friends, drugs, theft, wild dress to go with even wilder behavior. Why? Our other children, although not perfect, had never caused us any serious problems.

Unable to control the tears, I thought about all the chances we had given our son. He had run away from home at sixteen. We'd taken him back again and again only to have him abuse our trust and disrupt our family life. We had done all we knew to do until finally, tonight, my husband had to demand that he leave our home.

I wasn't prepared for a prodigal. I never imagined that one night I would lie in bed wondering where my son was. But once you love, you are never free again.

In looking back, I realize that the Lord allowed these difficult years and this trying situation to teach me many things.

I had to cope with overwhelming sadness that at times almost engulfed me. I had carried this child, given birth to him, cradled him in my arms, watched over him when he was sick, fixed his meals, washed his clothes, prayed for him and with him. After years of our giving all we had to this beloved child, he chose to disregard his training and reject his teaching.

Then came the guilt. During those first few months and many times afterward, I experienced stabs of guilt and searing self-doubt. Could I have brought him up differently? Had I been too strict—or not strict enough? Had I shown enough love? Had I truly gone the extra mile? Had I prayed enough? I knew I had made mistakes, but I also knew that I had done my best. Sadly, there were some Christians who made remarks or looked at me in a way that made these feelings all the more difficult. However, this taught me to be more sensitive to others going through similar experiences. We need to be approachable and available, not condemning. Showing love and concern.

At times the Lord had gently reminded me to deal with my son as He deals with His children: to keep the doors of communication always open, to accept the person, even when I could not accept his actions and conduct.

But as painful as it was, Stephan and I also realized we could not allow the behavior of this one child to consume us. At times we had to purposefully put our prodigal out of our minds. It simply wasn't fair to focus all our attention and emotional energy on him at the expense of the other members of the family.

Sometimes accomplishing this was terribly difficult. We had to ask the Lord for His wisdom and discernment in knowing how to demonstrate love to our son without approving of his behavior. The Lord reminded me that sometimes love has to be tough. Sometimes lessons are only learned the hard way. So I also had to be careful not to interfere with God's dealings in our son's life, allowing him to suffer the consequences of his choices and actions—even though my mother's heart wanted to shield him.

I also had to deal with repeated disappointment. My emotions felt as if they'd been jerked along on a carnival ride. Up. Down. High. Low. Soaring. Crashing. From time to time the situation seemed improved, the tensions less, my son's attitude different. I was encouraged and my hopes rose—hopes that he would keep his job, go back to school, be sorry, change his ways, even come home again. But soon we would experience yet another disappointment. As the years came and went I often found myself discouraged. I rode the waves of hope only to have my emotions crashed on the rocks of disappointment till I was battered and bruised.

Although there was really nothing else I could do during this troubled time, I often found it difficult to trust the Lord. I found myself wondering why God gave this boy parents if He didn't want us to be in charge. I was tempted again and again to do God's job for Him and would try my best to do something—anything—to help God out. I would interfere, manipulate, scheme, and even attempt to control the situation. My mother's heart ached for Tullian. I wanted to protect him. But it didn't help. It only frustrated and fragmented the family.

Several years passed. One Sunday, unknown to us, Tullian and his girlfriend came to church. At the end of the service, unexpectedly, Tullian took his girlfriend by the hand, and from high in the balcony, they went forward to give their lives to Jesus Christ.

I was overwhelmed with joy—but I must admit also a bit skeptical. I didn't want to have my hopes dashed again. I waited and watched. As the weeks turned into months, we saw this young man grow and mature into a sincere, dedicated child of God.

We have since celebrated Tullian's marriage to his lovely Kim, and now with two little sons of their own, they are in seminary preparing for ministry.

It is not attention that the child is seeking but love.

SIGMUND FREUD

Pierced Heart

Julie works for a Christian organization where families and family values rank high. Due to her position, her "image" is important. But having teenagers in the home who don't fit the traditional "youth group kid" mold has been a challenge for her. She loves her teens dearly but struggles with their choices of clothing and music.

I have to confess that if I didn't work where I do, I probably wouldn't get so uptight about some of these things. But the conservative organization I work for expects the whole family to get involved in picnics, projects, and other social functions. This would be just fine if my teens looked and acted more like the other employees' kids. But unfortunately (for me), my teens, especially my middle son, Sam, have some very different ideas.

My oldest boy went through his own phase, but he seems to have settled down some and is just starting community college. My youngest son, although no choirboy, is staying out of trouble and pulling average grades in middle school. But who knows what will happen next year or next week. Then there's Sam. This kid seems to thrive on shocking people. Maybe it's because he's in a rock band. Or maybe it's just his way of saying, "Look at me!" Whatever it is, I didn't think my friends at work were ready for it.

I suppose I could look into a different occupation, but the truth is I really like my job, and the benefits are great. I just wish the company didn't make such a big deal about families all the time. But then that's their image, the way they've always been and always will be. And it sure doesn't help that the CEO's kids are all doing just great—honor society, youth group, athletics—dream kids, it seems. In fact, some days when I get to work, it seems like every minivan and SUV in the employee parking lot has a bumper sticker proclaiming, "My kid's on the honor roll at Jefferson Middle School." Some mornings I almost can't take it.

But here's the really ironic part: My job includes a lot of traveling around the country, helping to coordinate seminars that teach about things like marriage, raising kids, and families. We address a lot of common problems, but it's always from the "we'll show you how to do this" angle. And sometimes I feel like a hypocrite as I chat with people and promote products that promise to help their families be "better." It's not that I don't believe in what we're doing; I know the things we teach really work for many, if not most, families. But they just don't seem to work for mine. And I always wonder what some mom might think if my own kids popped in right as I was telling her about my company's latest family video.

Well, this hit home in a big way just recently. I was coming home from a trip, along with some other employees. Our conversations usually seem to focus on our kids and families, especially when we're headed home. One woman in particular had been chatting with me about all these great college scholarships her daughter had been offered recently. When she asked me about Sam, who's in the same grade as her daughter, I just made a little joke about Sam's procrastinating ways and let her keep on talking. (I make a good listener when it comes to kids because I don't usually want to talk about my own.)

We finally got to our destination, gathered up our stuff, and headed off the plane. I was expecting my husband, Phil, to meet me, since he usually does. But as soon as I reached the gate, I spotted Sam and his friend Leo. Leo was sporting his usual spiked hair with aqua blue tips, but today he'd also outlined his lips with black pencil. I won't even go into his clothes, but suffice it to say they grab your attention. And then there was Sam with his dark shoulder-length hair (we decided long ago to fight only the important battles), wearing his normal odd assortment of clothes (a cross between bum and disco). But here's the clincher: From about thirty feet away I noticed right off that he'd pierced his lower lip in three different places. Between two large silver rings (which resemble fangs), a big stud glistened proudly in the center. Sam waved and my stomach sank. I thought I saw a cocky smirk in his eye, and I wondered if he'd done this just to embarrass me. And for a moment, I considered pretending I didn't even know these weird-looking kids.

I quickly glanced at my fellow employees, wondering if they were aware that these two strange young men had come to pick me up. But they seemed not to notice. And suddenly I knew I was being ridiculous—this was, after all, my son. So I shot up a quick silent prayer for strength and grace and bid my colleagues good-bye as I walked slowly over to Sam and Leo. I could feel my cheeks burning in humiliation, certain that everyone was staring at the three of us in horror. But I mentally chastised myself again and forced myself to throw my arms around my son in a big hug. I knew he was surprised by this act of public affection. Then I stepped back and looked directly at his lower lip and said, "Man, Sam, that must've really hurt." He looked at me curiously and kind of grinned as he picked up my bag. "Yeah, I thought you'd like it," he said sarcastically.

But now, here's the really surprising part of all this. On the following Monday, one of my coworkers who'd seen Sam at the airport pulled me aside. "I need to talk to you," Shelly whispered. As it turns out, she also has a son who's pushing the limits. And she was impressed with how I had greeted my son without any show of embarrassment. I quickly set her straight on that account. Then I told her I figured my most important job was to love my kids, and if it meant I put my day job at risk, well, so be it. And since then another mom has approached me, and we've begun a little support group of sorts. Sure, there are only three of us so far. But it's better than feeling all alone. Besides, I suspect our numbers will increase before long since a lot of the employees' kids haven't even hit their teens yet!

When Hope Dies

Louise is in her seventies now. But when she thinks of her son David, it seems as if it all happened just yesterday. They say time heals all wounds, but Louise admits that some pain never goes away completely. And while she has learned to move on with her life, and does so beautifully, there are still days when she feels blue.

David was the oldest of four beautiful children, two boys followed by two girls: your perfect baby-boomer family. And so we were. We lived in a beautiful home overlooking the Golden Gate Bridge. Our children were intelligent, attractive, and highly motivated. Okay, to be honest, they made us proud—very proud. We were the quintessential all-American family. But then the sixties and seventies came along, and our lives began to unravel.

David had been class president and graduated as valedictorian in 1968. And although he received many excellent offers from prestigious schools across the country, he decided to take advantage of a full scholarship at Stanford. He planned to major in political science, and his future looked extremely bright. And why shouldn't it?

During his first year of college, however, things began to change. The first thing we noticed was that he stopped calling or coming home. But why should we worry? This was our golden boy—the one with the Midas touch. We knew he was doing just fine—probably just too busy with classes and social activities. Besides, we were busily involved with our other children. It was Kevin's senior year now, and the girls were both in junior high. We had our hands full living out the American dream.

Then David came home for Christmas. He'd grown a beard and let his hair grow. He wore the worn and patched clothing so characteristic of the hippie era we'd just entered. We weren't quite sure what to think but decided not to make too big of a deal. And then David assured us that he was simply on a journey toward "enlightenment." He wanted to "find himself." We had never for a moment considered him lost.

By spring, David's grades had slipped to the point where he was placed on academic probation. And when I went to Stanford to meet with an academic counselor, I was informed that they suspected that David, like many of his peers, was experimenting with drugs. Our David? We couldn't believe it. But when we confronted him with this information, he looked us in the eye and admitted it was true. "It's my way of finding out who I am and what I need to do in this life," he said. And that's when he announced that he was leaving school and embarking on a "mind-expanding" journey that he hoped would lead him to himself.

For several years David lived in numerous countries. He traveled in the Far East, hiked the Himalayas, and even dwelled with Indians in Peru. He diligently studied with the various gurus and spiritual "wise men" of the era. And during this time, he continued to experiment with drugs—mostly the "mind-expanding" varieties, the hallucinogens. But it became increasingly clear to all who knew him that LSD was his favorite—his drug of choice. He admitted to close friends that he had "tripped out" on LSD hundreds, maybe even thousands, of times.

Despite his drug use, David still managed to do some amazing things with his life. He painstakingly built a beautiful log cabin with his own tools, but he later burned it down (because it was constructed on public lands). He wrote poetry and songs that still make me cry. He even fathered a darling little boy. And somehow, despite what he was doing to his mind, his soul remained intact, beautiful even. But his search for spiritual peace was relentless.

No matter how hard his family tried to help or rescue him from his self-destructive lifestyle, he wouldn't allow us to intervene. He felt certain he was still on the path of spiritual enlightenment, determined to go wherever it led.

David ended his earthly life on his younger brother's front lawn, dousing himself with gasoline and then striking a fatal match. Kevin never fully recovered from the shock and loss that day. None of us has. It was as if hope died with David.

Our son's life and death have affected our world in ways we cannot share or describe. Sometimes it seems like all we have left are the memories. I try to focus on the happy ones—his earlier life, his brilliant achievements, his sincerity, his hunger for truth. For those are the only pieces I have left to hold. The rest I must entrust into the hands of my loving heavenly Father. In his divine embrace hope might resurrect itself once more. For I know that with God all things are possible.

And so I revive my hope, and I pray to God that I will see my son again someday—whole and happy and finally found at last!

An Encouraging Word

GIGI GRAHAM TCHIVIDJIAN

It was a warm, balmy north Florida evening. The waves gently lapped the white sand beach outside of our hotel room, and the palm fronds rustled against the window as we dressed for dinner.

Mother was to be interviewed at an event honoring a prestigious medical institution. During the interview she answered questions about her childhood in China, her high school years in North Korea, and then her marriage to, and her life with, my daddy, Billy Graham. She went on to discuss her years as a mother; her joys as well as her difficulties. She talked about the times of having to make decisions when Daddy was away preaching, sometimes tough decisions, alone. She also shared about the trying, difficult years when she had to deal with her prodigals.

After dinner, many came up to speak and to thank her for her honest, open sharing. I noticed one distinguished, well-dressed woman who hung back, waiting for a chance to speak. Tension was evident and she struggled to hold back the tears. When the crowd cleared, she approached Mother timidly, hesitantly. "My son died of an overdose of drugs," she said with difficulty. "Do you think I will see him again in heaven?"

Of course, Mother didn't know any of the details, but she saw before her a mother with a very heavy heart. So she answered. "If you heard a timid knock on your door one day, and you answered the knock only to find your child standing there, bruised, wounded, bleeding, dirty, and tattered, what would you do? Slam the door in his face? Or would you throw open the door and welcome him into your arms?"

Suddenly, this mother's face registered relief. I saw the load lift from her shoulders as the tears flowed down her cheeks because she knew she was hearing from a mother who knew what it was like to have a prodigal. They hugged each other, and the woman turned and disappeared into the crowd.

On the Way There

LINDA

Steam rises,
a litany of manholes, pleading
all along Thirteenth Avenue at 2 A.M.
Taverns' neon signs glitter with old raindrops,
but the drunks outside don't notice: they're busy,
singing.

I drive on,
toward the ER. If he's already gone,
what will I do, I ask the air,
which has that moldy smell
this city gets at night.
The drunks sing another verse.

Automatic doors jolt me
a little past alertness;
piece by piece I enter the room.
If it's too late, he's still my son.
Please, please.
The only prayer I know.

Refuge

A MOTHER'S PRAYER

Heavenly Father,

How I wish I could still protect my children from accident and disease; from the wrong crowd and bad decisions; from all the daily threats to body, mind, soul, and spirit that are part of our world.

But I can't.

So, Father, I kneel before you today in great need. Only you can see my children every moment. You can send your angels as ministering spirits to guard them. Your everlasting arms can lift them up above all dangers. Your Spirit can whisper to them, "Not that way—this way. Walk here."

Please do that for my son today. And as for me, let me bask in the peace that comes from trusting you alone.

Amen.

IS THIS ALL
MY FAULT?

LINDA

I tell my friends I'm convinced I invented guilt. I think it started on the delivery table when I gave birth to my first son. The doctor yelled, "It's a boy!" and I immediately apologized for dirtying up the sheets, swearing at the charge nurse, and biting my husband on the hand during transition. Guilt followed me home from the hospital, and it has been hanging around ever since.

The late Erma Bombeck wrote that guilt is the gift that keeps on giving. While dads undoubtedly suffer twinges of remorse too—say after Junior takes pop's new car out for a spin and flattens a stop sign—guilt is more often the territory of moms. Mothers are guilt experts—both in giving and receiving. Those of us with lost boys get lots of practice.

We moms are practically the embodiment of guilt itself. Does the baby have a runny nose? Mom didn't bundle him up enough. Did little Johnny flunk his spelling test? She forgot to drill him on those words one last time. Is middle-aged son late on his car payment? Ma must have failed to teach him how to write out a check.

A standing joke in my family is that whatever happens—be it a catastrophic flood or a pair of lost socks—it's mom's fault. I used to get frustrated with the way the kids casually expected me to understand their logic. If they were late, I hadn't awakened them early enough. If I pulled open the blinds to rouse them earlier, I was a cruel prison matron. In their minds even the dog could trace the cause of a bad flea day to me. I couldn't win.

When my boys began to get themselves into more serious scrapes than just being late to class, my guilt began to grow proportionally. I fretted over everything. There weren't enough hours in the day to handle my aching conscience. Once I even dreamed I missed out on eternal blessings because I arrived in heaven with guilt baggage that wouldn't fit in the overhead compartment. All the while my boys (and the dog) skipped through life without so much as a fanny pack of remorse for their mistakes.

When one of your boys takes a detour in life, you might say, "Well, Jason's a mess, but just look at Ronnie." But when more than one of your sons keeps you up nights worrying about everything from their safety to whether the family valuables are still intact, people may hint that your parenting skills need some polishing. When all your boys are in trouble of one sort or another, it seems there's no way to avoid the guilty verdict. The question is, Where does the guilt end?

No matter who tries to tell me I'm not to blame for other people's actions, I'm always dreaming up ways to improve as a mom. Every time I try to stop feeling responsible for my kids' troubles, I feel as if I'm on a treadmill that just goes on and on.

For example, my oldest, who has kept things interesting since he was five minutes old, amazes me with his capacity to invent new ways to shock both his loved ones and his prospective employers. He's gotten tickets for skateboarding, uprooted city trees while intoxicated, and cursed at a municipal judge. The judge didn't take the last one very well. My son has become familiar with something called "Road Crew" and has had to pay lots of fines. He says it's hard being the oldest; you have to do everything before the rest of the kids. I tell him it's even harder being the mom because, no matter what, I know it's all my fault.

Son number two has the scourge of being the middle child. He reminds me, usually every ten minutes, how difficult his position in the birth order is. Middle boy has some real and challenging problems. He's the one who has panic attacks and hasn't been to a regular school since sixth grade. You guessed it: I wake up in the night worried that it's all because of that time he fell over in his walker.

Son three was a preemie—the one who had trouble nursing. You know what that means. It's amazing that poor boy has survived at all, what with the lack of natural immunities in baby formula.

Do I feel guilty about all of this? Of course. Are my sons' transgressions my fault? You betcha. Am I different from most mothers on the planet? I don't think so.

To be sure, a lot of mom guilt is self-imposed. But when you're a mom of a lost boy, aren't things bad enough without heaping coals upon your own head?

A lot of the time I think I equate guilt with love. As long as I'm trying to rescue my sons, I'm convinced I'm showing my love for them. I get so intertwined with their lives that I can't tell where I end and they begin. But...what if I step back and let God do the worrying?

I wonder how Jesus' mom might have handled it. I doubt Mary berated herself because she forgot to tell Jesus to take an extra cloak or felt inadequate because her son got lost in the temple. I think Mary trusted God and didn't waste her time feeling guilty over everything that happened.

Maybe it's time for moms like us to learn from Mary. Guilt trips just trip us up. The less time we spend stumbling over stones of guilt, the more we're free to let real love flow. And that's a gift no one can afford to pass up.

———

No one can make you feel inferior without your consent.

E l e a n o r R o o s e v e l t

Getting Off the Guilt-Go-Round

Bob and Donna Stewart's second son, Ryan, has mild autism. His frequent outbursts and unique needs make it difficult for the Stewarts to maintain consistent discipline with their four children, and sometimes the other kids resent the special attention sixteen-year-old Ryan receives at home. Donna struggles to be fair but often feels guilty about the situation.

I'm just like any mom: I love all my children. My husband, Bob, and I try to be fair, whether it's about chores, allowances, or discipline. But because of Ryan's special needs, it isn't always possible to give our other kids equal time or to be completely egalitarian in enforcing rules.

Every mother knows it's hard to be fair to all your kids all the time. That's been one of the most difficult things our family has faced. Because of Ryan's disability, he does get more than his share of the attention—even if it's mostly negative attention. Most of the time seventeen-year-old Jeff, ten-year-old Ben, and fourteen-year-old Lindsay don't complain, but eventually somebody gets upset—and then we argue about why Mom and Dad give Ryan special treatment.

Jeff knows this all too well. He wonders why it appears that so much more is required of him than is required of Ryan. "It's always about Ryan," he says.

One day Jeff suddenly announced he didn't want to go to Sunday morning church services anymore. He plays high-school soccer and gets exhausted from all the games and practices; he wanted to sleep in on Sundays. Bob and I told him our rule was that he had to attend with us until he was eighteen. He immediately shot back, "Then why doesn't Ryan have to go?"

Jeff knows Ryan has a difficult time in a crowded place like church. Getting ready on time is a huge challenge for his younger brother too. Jeff also knows that bringing up fairness pushes my guilt buttons. Right away I felt awful about the double standard. After some arguing, we finally met each other halfway. Jeff agreed to attend services on Wednesday nights instead of Sunday mornings. Jeff's good at compromise, and I was proud of the way he was willing to negotiate, but the situation still didn't answer his question of why we have different expectations of Ryan.

The fact is, I count on my other children to behave responsibly when I'm so busy "putting out fires" with Ryan. His form of autism, Asperger's syndrome, is a type that allows him to function well a lot of the time, but he's unpredictable. I never know when he's going to have a bad day. I think Jeff, Ben, and Lindsay sometimes act out as a way of saying, "Pay attention to us too." Those are the times when there is too little of me to go around. And of course, I tell myself I should be doing a better job.

Lindsay takes it the hardest. She's a high achiever—straight-A student, involved in school sports and church youth group, the works. Most of the time she's wonderful. But she gets especially defensive if she occasionally breaks a house rule and is disciplined. She'll react by saying, "But I do practically everything right! Why doesn't Ryan get in trouble when he does the same thing?"

Lindsay knows what we'll say. "But we can't punish him. Your brother requires a different style of discipline than you or Ben or Jeff."

"It's so not fair!" Lindsay always yells back. And I have to agree. I'm always tempted to throw in the old saw about life not being fair, but I doubt that would make her feel any better.

Even Ben, who shares a room with Ryan, notices inconsistencies. He's only ten, but he's tried some of the things he sees his brother get away with—like pretending he didn't hear me ask him to empty the trash. Ben says, "Ry never has to do stuff—why should I?"

I'm up to my ears in guilt because I don't have an easy answer. I want to be consistent with all my children, but Ryan has a disability. Simple as that. God wouldn't expect him to walk if he were in a wheelchair or to see things if he were blind. Ryan has to do things at his own pace.

I could reverse the guilt trip and tell Ben to be thankful he doesn't have Ryan's problems. I could remind Lindsay that she isn't the only girl with a special-needs brother. And I could guilt Jeff into being a part of the solution, not part of the problem. The thing is, they know that stuff. But it doesn't make their hurt feelings go away.

They also know guilt can be a good thing. It's necessary if we're talking about a serious crime. Yet the kind of guilt that sits on a whole family like a heavy wet blanket can't be healthy. I don't want my children learning to manufacture their own false guilt.

I'm working on reversing the trend and learning to accept the blame only for problems that are truly my own. Sometimes this process is painful, as when I feel guilty for something Ryan does because I think I should be able to control him. Other times it's hilarious, as when I blame myself for not predicting sudden rain. I have to get off the guilt-go-round, and I know I'll need God's help to do it.

After a few Sundays of sleeping in, Jeff decided he needed to be with his youth group more than he needed the extra rest. "Ry says he wants to come with me," he added. My guilt melted away, and I hugged him.

It isn't easy to change, but I'm praying for wisdom and courage as well as asking my family to stop me when I start blaming myself for everything. We're all doing the best we can, I tell them. That's all God expects of anybody, isn't it?

====

The truth is the kindest thing we can give folks in the end.

H ARRIET B EECHER S TOWE

Breaking the Ice

Kelli was raised in a fairly conservative family with older parents who rarely if ever discussed issues relating to sex. As a result she experienced difficulties bringing up these "delicate" subjects with her own teenage son. And being a single mom didn't help the matter. Finally she reached her wit's end when she discovered a large box of condoms in her son's bedroom.

I started getting nervous when I sensed Ricky was approaching puberty. His father and I had just split up, and knowing my ex and his irresponsible ways, I suspected it would be up to me to have that "little talk" with my son. And yet I had no idea where to begin. You see, my parents were close to forty when they had me, and I think my very conventional mother would rather have been beaten with a stick than to discuss the facts of life with me or anyone. And I'm sure this has affected the way I parent my son.

But to be perfectly honest, chatting with Ricky about the birds and the bees wasn't exactly at the top of my priority list either. I was scared to be on my own and suddenly responsible for all our finances. I began working overtime at my job just to make ends meet. I do remember telling Ricky that he'd have to take on more responsibilities too, that he'd have to become the "man" of the house. Maybe he just took me a little too literally.

Before I knew it, Ricky was sixteen and, I thought, a perfectly normal kid. Which as it turns out he was! But I had no idea that he was toying with the idea of becoming sexually active at that time. I mean it's not like your kids come home and announce these things— at least mine didn't. And I suppose I was being something of an ostrich with my head in the sand—the old ignorance is bliss sort of thing. But honestly, I think I actually believed that Ricky's relation- ships with girls were purely platonic. I mean this was a kid who did his homework, brought home good grades, went to church—why would he think it was okay to have sex?

Duh? I guess I don't watch enough television and movies. Or read teen magazines. If I'd been a little more aware, I'm sure I would've realized that the chances of my son's having sex as a teenager were greater than not. My little ignorant era ended one day just before Ricky turned seventeen.

I had an unexpected day off and, to be nice, decided to do his laundry (he'd been doing it himself for years). I took a neat basket of clean, folded clothes into his room, and instead of setting it on his bed, I decided to be really nice and put things away.

You can imagine my surprise when I opened his sock drawer to find a giant-sized box of condoms—and a number of them were missing! I felt as if someone had just jolted me with a thousand watts! I stared at the box in horror, unsure of what I should do. Confiscate the box? Well, then what would I do if Ricky got some girl pregnant? But what if he did anyway? And what about sexually transmitted dis- eases? And what about—

I couldn't take it anymore. I just sat down on his bed and cried. Then I began to blame myself. If only I'd had that sex talk with him. Or if I had been home more, instead of working all those extra hours.

Then I blamed his father. If only he hadn't left us just as Ricky was hitting puberty. And finally, I just sat there and poured my heart out to God. I begged him to give me wisdom, to show me how to handle this situation without destroying the good relationship I thought I already had with my son. His father had been so absent during the past two years that I knew Ricky looked to me for everything. I couldn't attack him about this and risk destroying our bond.

Finally, feeling somewhat calmed (but still shaken) I left the box of condoms right where it was and went to wait for him to come home from track practice. When Ricky walked in the door, he could tell something was wrong. I could see the concern on his face, and I decided to cut right to the chase.

"Ricky, I was putting some clean laundry away in your room, and I happened to notice a box of condoms." I think those were the hardest words I've spoken to my son. I watched as splotches of red crept up his neck and into his cheeks. But he didn't appear angry. "I didn't mean to snoop," I continued, "but I couldn't help but wonder if this doesn't mean you've decided to become sexually active"—(more tough words for me)—"and this really concerns me."

Now I could see that Ricky's embarrassment was quickly changing to anger, and I really didn't want this to turn into a confrontation. I prayed silently as we both stood there, face to face, and then I said, "Ricky, it's just because I love you that I'm concerned. And, well, I feel kind of guilty that I never sat down and talked with you about all this…this stuff"—now I started to cry—"when you were younger."

"Aw, Mom, it's not your fault," said Ricky, his dark brown eyes now focused on the floor. "I've known all about that stuff for ages."

"But you never heard about it from me," I tried to explain. "I never took the time to tell you how I think it's really important that you save sex until marriage. I never told you that it scares me to think you might get some disease or maybe get a girl pregnant—"

"Mom," he interrupted with irritation, "that's why I use protection. Jeez!"

"I know, I know. But that's not always enough. You don't understand—"

"Yes, I do. They teach this stuff at school. There's nothing you can tell me that I don't know. I haven't even done it that many times, and I'm real careful." He turned away and began heading to his room.

"But you don't know everything," I called out weakly. "Condoms really aren't 100 percent foolproof, Ricky."

"Just give it a rest, Mom." He was at his door now.

"But, Ricky,"—I bit my lip, wondering if I could really say the next sentence—"your father was using a condom when I got pregnant with you."

He stopped with his hand on the door and slowly turned. "Really?"

I knew I had his attention. At that moment of truth my son came back, and we talked openly about everything for the first time ever. And I told him how I felt, what I expected from him, where God absolutely drew the line. But I also told him that I knew he'd make his own choice and that all I could do was pray he'd make the right one. Then I asked him to talk with our youth pastor about all this. And to my amazement he promised me he would.

I still feel guilty for not bringing all this up sooner. But I realize there's no sense beating myself up now. At least the communication doors between me and my son are wide open. And I don't think I'll ever let them get shut again.

Seesaw Parents

Larry and Kathy had already raised the children from each of their first marriages with distinctly different parenting styles. All five of the kids became successful adults. Peter, the son they had together, was a "December baby." Like many boys, he began to rebel when he reached middle-school age. When Peter began to fail his classes and experiment with marijuana, both parents thought they knew exactly how to straighten out their son. That's when Larry and Kathy began to have problems of their own.

L arry and I don't fight very often—we both had enough arguing in our first marriages. But when it came to Peter, we had a hard time agreeing on anything. The more Peter got into trouble, the more my husband and I were at odds with one another. The turmoil brought our marriage to its knees.

We were thrilled when Peter arrived. Even though I was in my forties, he was born healthy and had a head of thick black hair. He was smart and funny when he was a little boy. Larry and I adored him. His brothers and sisters, all grown and on their own, treated him like a little prince. I guess he was a little spoiled, but Peter was never a problem. I thought the worst thing we had to deal with was Pete's allergies and his stubborn refusal to drink soy milk.

Like a lot of seventh-grade boys, Peter started testing his teachers and acting out in class. He wouldn't do any homework and tried to convince us that the school was at fault. We put him in a private school, but he continued his antics. When we caught him smoking pot behind the garage, we knew we had to do something.

Trouble is, Larry and I couldn't agree on what that something should be. I had raised my kids with strict discipline, and no excuses were good enough. I expected my kids to "toe the line" as my own mom had taught me. I was pretty unyielding when it came to rules and consequences.

Larry had a much different upbringing. He is more easygoing and open in his approach. He allowed his kids more freedom than I was comfortable with and wanted Peter to have the same free rein. When I'd point out Peter's infraction, Larry would defend him, excusing his behavior for one reason or another.

I disliked Larry's relaxed methods as much as he disapproved of my ideas on child rearing. He called me "the Warden" if I tried to hold Pete to a consequence. He maintained that I was too strict; my harsh discipline would drive Peter into far worse things. I think we both knew that our divisiveness was damaging, but we were so stubborn. And both of us were so sure we were right.

Our deepest fear was that because we couldn't agree, our son's problems were really our fault. I began to think about separating from Larry. After many failed attempts to work things out, we decided to get counseling.

In the counseling office we heard the same advice over and over: As long as Peter knew we weren't acting in unison, he'd take advantage of it. "United we stand, divided we fall," the counselor said. We love Peter and want the best for him, and the counselor helped us make a list of ways to compromise.

We thought we were making progress. I bit my tongue when Larry reasoned with Peter. Larry stopped calling me the Warden. But Peter's problems began to get more serious. He was arrested for spray-painting on a school building. He received a fine and probation and still wasn't doing well at school. The situation got more and more stressful.

We were losing Peter because of our poor parenting techniques. I doubted myself and decided maybe Larry had been right all along: Strict discipline wasn't the answer. I didn't know it at the time, but Larry was starting to think that in order to control Pete, perhaps *he* should turn into the Warden. Before we knew what was happening, Larry and I began to switch roles.

Peter was totally confused by our strange role reversal. For a while Pete didn't do anything out of order; I think he was scared Larry and I were aliens that had replaced his real parents. Instead of my yelling for stricter rules, there was Larry acting like Mr. Tough Guy. I was having long chats with Pete, making excuses for him to Larry. Peter couldn't play his usual victim role with either one of us.

After a time Pete returned to his unacceptable behavior. The last week of eighth grade he got caught lighting a bunch of sparklers in the boys' bathroom. He was suspended and not allowed to attend the graduation party. The worst part for me was in the principal's office, where Pete blurted out, "It's all my mom's fault. One day she's like a cop, and then she acts like a friend. It's scary." The principal raised her eyebrows at me but said nothing. Inside, though, I knew something had to change.

The first thing I decided to do was to pray. God already knew Larry and I loved Pete and did our best to raise him well. I began to ask God for parenting guidance daily, and it has helped me to feel more confident in my parenting. God is teaching me to try not to react harshly to Peter but also to stay consistent.

Next I told Pete where I stood. "The really scary thing," I said, "will be if you continue to act out and get into serious trouble. No judge is going to excuse you because your mom messed up. Your behavior is your responsibility."

Last, I told my husband that I would back him up in whatever he did to discipline Peter. "I promise not to interfere from now on," I said. "Peter needs to stop getting mixed signals." Larry's and my relationship is much better as we pull together to raise our son.

Pete is still going through some things. I occasionally still act like the Warden. But Larry and I don't fight over Pete as much anymore. We've learned that seesaw parents aren't good for children or marriages.

One Week After

LINDA

Who can sleep on a mattress tilted upon its side,
wear clothes now piled into garbage bags
even though they lay strewn like land mines
all those years?

Did I say
we ought to rid ourselves
of such ungrateful offspring,
after he spewed spit and epithets
for the umpteenth time?

We thought we had the answer;
together we tossed him out.
He wouldn't toe the line
and he got the tough side of our love.

This is the bed we've made and today unmade.
Stripped of a son's *Star Wars* sheets
and drool-stained pillow
we cannot sleep tonight.

A Promise of Renewal

Dear Father,

Sometimes it seems that my failures as a mom, more than my successes, have shaped how my son thinks and feels, what he wants for his life, and who he's become.

Forgive me, Lord. Have mercy on me for every way that I have brought harm rather than good to him. Show me any way that I can make amends—and help me to do so right away. By your grace, redeem every hurt for your glory.

Now help me to let go of the kind of guilt that is only debilitating because it doesn't lead to repentance and growth. Help me to see where my part ends and your part and my son's own choices begin.

I know I could have done better, but I'm even more certain that you, loving Father, are still at work for good in my son's life and in mine.

Amen.

WHEN "SUCCESSFUL" PARENTS INQUIRE

LINDA

I'm sure you've been there. You run into an old friend, one you haven't seen for years. It's bad enough that she still looks terrific—she asks you how things are going with your boys. You suck in your stomach, straighten your shoulders. You know you're going to have to tell her something.

She says her Josh is up for a scholarship and little Matt just took honors at the gymnastics meet. She goes on about how great her guys are, how she never dreamed they'd do so well. You nod, trying your best not to think bad thoughts about your friend or her offspring. You say something generic, like "Oh that's fantastic." Perhaps you manage a smile. After an uncomfortable pause, she asks, "So how are *your* kids?"

My husband, Brad, tells me I should say nothing when friends and acquaintances ask about our kids. "Just say we're fine," he says. "Fine." It's nobody's business if we have problems. His motto is, Let 'em wonder.

My usual approach in such situations is kind of like Brad's motto:

Say nothing unless pressed. If pressed, smile wide, be as vague as possible, and maintain a cheery tone. "Oh, gee, they're...teenagers, ya know?"

Hey, I figure I'm about as honest as the next embarrassed mom. Or so I thought until last week.

I was in the grocery store with my son Nate and his girlfriend, Naomi. This wasn't so awful—my son and his girl are nice enough people. The problem (for me) was that Naomi had dyed her hair magenta (again) and Nate sported three new piercings—metallic studs protruded from both his temples as well as between his brows. Shoppers gawked at us, and I began to wish I'd worn a ski mask and Groucho glasses. We waited in the checkout line, and I tried to slump further down into my parka.

Nate and Naomi chatted happily, as if they were daring folks to say something. People stared, and I edged as far away from my son as I could. Then I felt a tap on my shoulder.

A former neighbor stood there, the sort that sends you her family's Christmas newsletter for years after they move away. "It's so good to see you!" she chirped. My stomach lurched as I remembered those annual brag sheets—full of boastings about her family. She'd always made it sound as if all her children were destined to win the Nobel Prize. I looked around for a quick exit, but I was trapped between shopping carts.

"So how are *your* little ones?" She craned her neck to see who was with me. She'd moved away when my kids were still in primary school. Back then they were just rough-and-tumble regular little boys, and jewelry was for sissies. The only hardware Nate wore then was his GI Joe dog tag.

The woman put on her glasses, squinted, and gasped. "Why that's not Nathaniel, is it? Good grief, he's got nails sticking straight out of his head." Nate was still preoccupied with Naomi. Light glinted off his temples whenever he moved.

I wanted to tell her how it is, how it's been—years of problems with drugs, alcohol, and now body piercings that give me a headache when I look at them. I longed to say, "Everything's a mess" or even, "Life stinks." I wanted to tell the truth. But I didn't.

I forced a laugh and looked over at Nate to make sure he was still engrossed in conversation with Naomi. Then a terrible thing happened. I heard myself say, "Oh no. That's not my son." As soon as I said it, my stomach knotted, and I was sure lightning would strike me dead.

My former neighbor looked relieved and winked conspiratorially. "Why, in our day," she said, clucking her tongue for emphasis, "kids didn't look like walking pin cushions, did they?" Then she said something else about airport metal detectors, but I hardly heard her. I was too busy trying to make myself invisible.

I left the woman wondering about my son and my family, but I felt even worse about denying my relationship with my son. *What if God took that approach with me?*

The truth is, there are days when I simply can't face the problems, when listening to someone else's success is more than I can take. Inevitably, those days are the same ones I meet someone who asks questions I can't bear to answer.

But here's the rub: If all of us moms whose sons are in trouble try to appear as if everything's peachy, then what do we have? A lot of lonely, shame-filled moms who think everyone else's boys are "fine."

Later it occurred to me that I was so embarrassed by Nate in the store that I forgot to ask about my former neighbor's boys, who would also be teenagers by now. Maybe she was dying to meet someone today who would say, "My boys are having trouble too. Isn't it hard?"

I'm not saying we should air our dirty laundry every chance we get, but if we moms won't admit the truth about our sons, much less that they *are* our sons, we all run the risk of not being able to help each other when we need support the most.

The way I see it, when inquiring friends ask about our lost boys, we have three choices. We can let 'em wonder. We can tell a pretty lie dressed up in vagueness. Or we can take off our Groucho glasses and say, "Actually, he's having some trouble. Could you put us on your prayer list?"

―――――

He heals up the brokenhearted
And binds up their wounds.

P SALM 1 47:3

Saving the Lost

Mark and Laura Miller spent nearly twenty successful years on the mission field before the rebellion of their two teenage sons forced them to return home to the States early so that they could attempt to salvage what was left of their family.

I never dreamed anything like this could happen to us. After all, we'd succeeded at saving lost souls in a foreign country, but it seemed we'd failed miserably with our own two teenage sons. We returned home, feeling beaten and humiliated.

Mark and I were so embarrassed by the behavior of our boys that we weren't even sure we could show our faces back at the old mission base again. We worked in the field while our boys (only a year apart in age) attended the mission high school there. During this time both boys began to experiment with alcohol and cigarettes, then moved on to drugs (a shock to us since we thought we were living in a relatively "safe" environment). Most kids on base seemed stable, into academics, sports, and other wholesome activities. But somehow our boys' taste in music switched from Jars of Clay to Nine Inch Nails, and their physical appearances drastically changed into what many of the other missionary parents described as "Satanic" and revolting. Josh, our youngest son, pierced himself in numerous places, including his face. And Caleb, the older one, actually hitchhiked into the nearby town and got a tattoo. Both of these things were strictly for-bidden by the school, and both boys knew it. But their grades had already dropped by then, and it was just a matter of time anyway. Soon both our sons (then a sophomore and a junior) were perma-nently expelled from the mission high school.

It's hard to admit this, but Mark and I felt too embarrassed to return to our hometown in the States (where our local church had faithfully supported our family for almost two decades). I mean, how could we show up with these two little rebels by our side? So we decided to relocate temporarily to the other side of the country, using the mission's U.S. home base as an excuse for the choice. The truth is, we just couldn't bear to have our home congregation see us like that. Not only were we humiliated, but right or wrong, we suspected our Christian friends would judge us and our boys harshly. And we just couldn't handle that. Besides, we knew our sons needed our help and attention, and more than that, they needed our unconditional accep-tance and love. We were willing to do whatever it took to get Caleb and Josh back on track again.

So for the next few years Mark and I struggled to find jobs, and we got some good family counseling. It was a challenging and daily thing because we never knew from one day to the next if we'd be called into the school for a behavior problem or whatever. It's the hardest thing I've ever been through—much harder than going to the foreign mission field, even harder than childbirth! It's difficult to explain fully how tortured I felt during those years. And alone.

Even now, six years later, it's painful to remember all we went through. It just about destroyed our marriage. Sometimes Mark blamed me. Sometimes I blamed him. Sometimes we just fought over nothing in particular. Fortunately we did plug into a good church with an understanding pastor. Otherwise, I don't know if we would've made it at all.

But by the grace of God, we *did* make it. And amazingly our sons managed to emerge from their rocky coming of age without too many scars. I think it helped a lot that, despite how humiliated we were by their behavior, they knew we loved them and stood by them. We could hardly believe it when Josh removed his piercings to join the military. You can hardly see the marks now. And with his starched uniform and short haircut, you would never recognize him as the teen he used to be. And Caleb, to our complete amazement, has graduated from college and decided to follow in our footsteps by becoming a missionary!

When I look back on the toughest years of my life, I wish I'd done a few things differently. Mostly I wish I hadn't been so embarrassed by my sons' behavior. I wish I could have had the faith to recognize they were simply embarking on their own spiritual search. I know our humiliation as their parents only exacerbated an already difficult situation. After all, we knew that our sons were strong-willed young men who were determined to find themselves on their own terms. Why should we have been so embarrassed by that? I'm sure God doesn't get embarrassed every time I blow it!

If I could encourage a mom in a similar situation, I'd say just give it some time and prayer and don't wrap your personal identity so tightly into your children—for they are, after all, their own persons.

Rainbow Brite

Debbie is one of those women who delights in maintaining an orderly home and children who behave. And during their grade-school years, her kids seemed fairly easy and manageable. As a result, she and her husband, Tom, thought this whole parenting thing was a piece of cake. Consequently, Debbie confesses to having judged other parents. But she now admits that she was wrong about a lot of things.

I majored in education and taught school for several years before Tom and I decided to have children of our own. I'd always considered myself pretty good with kids, and I couldn't understand why some parents would complain so much about parenting being so hard. And when I saw kids that I thought were floundering, I would always blame the parents, thinking, *Well, if they'd just do this or that...their kids wouldn't act up so much.* I honestly thought I was an expert. I knew my kids would never do those kinds of things.

And for the first several years after our two boys were born, I held to these convictions. I ran a tight ship at home, and my boys pretty much toed the line. And I'm sure I derived a twisted sense of pride from the whole thing. Okay, I'll admit it: I was a control freak! It was terribly important for me to keep up appearances. I'm sure I never took my boys out in public unless their hair was combed and their clothes were clean and neat. And I enjoyed the compliments we got along the way.

We hit the preteen years in the early nineties. And suddenly, Todd, our oldest, no longer liked the clothing I picked out for him. He wanted to wear what he wanted to wear. And what he wanted to wear was (in my opinion) either really weird, too extreme, or just plain unattractive. And the same with the hair. Even when I'd insist he get a "traditional" haircut, he'd pull out the hair gel and manage to turn his hair into something that resembled a crazed porcupine. But as if that weren't bad enough, his little brother, Jeremy, began to follow in his footsteps.

Pretty soon it seemed like the only thing we talked about in our home was how the boys looked. And often it was in pretty loud voices too! But what really complicated things for me was how I was surrounded by friends and family and church people who'd come to expect our family to look and act a certain way. I expected it too! And suddenly I knew I was losing (or had lost) control over my boys. I was more than frustrated. I felt like I was holding back a tidal wave with an umbrella.

For a while I insisted that Todd and Jeremy tone down their hair and dress for church. Our church was pretty conservative, and I hadn't seen anyone else's teens dressed the way my boys wanted to dress. I suspected that word was getting around that our boys were turning into "little rebels"—the kind of kids I had always judged the parents for. And I figured it was only fair that I was about to get a dose of what I'd dished out (even if I'd never actually spoken the words). Remember what Jesus said about not judging others or we would be judged ourselves? Well, he was absolutely right.

One incident will always stand out in my mind. The boys were fifteen and thirteen at the time, and we'd left them home with a pizza and a video while Tom and I enjoyed a date night. It was after midnight when we got home, and both boys were already in bed (nice, but unusual). The next morning we got up late, and everyone was scrambling to get to church on time. I'd thrown some breakfast things on the table, then dashed back upstairs to get dressed. Finally we all hopped in the car for church. It was still winter and both boys had on hats. No big deal, except they know that Tom does not allow them to wear hats in church.

By the time we got to church I could hear the boys giggling in the backseat. No big deal; they still get silly sometimes. As we were hurrying toward the entrance of the church, Tom reminded them about the hat rule. At the front door, both boys got this really strange look on their faces, and then off came the hats. My eyes nearly popped out when I saw Todd's normally brown hair had somehow been transformed into what looked like lime green fuzz. And Jeremy was sporting stripes of lime green, bright blue, and magenta. My thirteen-year-old looked just like Rainbow Brite!

Tom and I were speechless (as was the elderly usher now holding the door for us). I looked at Tom in desperation. Do we go in? Or turn and run back to our car before anyone else sees us? Tom took a deep breath and nodded toward the church. Grimly, the four of us walked in. And what do you think the pastor's sermon was about that day? "Let he who is without sin cast the first stone."

Well, we left church in a hurry as soon as the last hymn was sung. And I can't honestly say that all our trials in regard to our boys' fashion choices were over after that. But it was a turning point of sorts.

Now I realize that kids just want to be themselves. And the harder we try as parents to force them into our tight little mold, the more likely they are to resist.

I've learned to lighten up and to let go of some of my controlling ways. I'm also learning not to worry so much about what other people think of us. Because the facts are, teens will be teens, and there's bound to be an embarrassing moment or ten along the way. The important thing is that our kids know we love them and accept them "as is." What more can a mother do?

───────

The worst loneliness is not to be comfortable with yourself.

MARK TWAIN

The Big Secret

As far as Eileen Morgan's friends and family know, her son, Rob, is a typical teenager with no serious problems. In fact, he's been arrested five times in three years—and he's only seventeen. Most of Rob's crimes are minor—curfew violations, being a minor in possession of alcohol and marijuana, skateboarding on private property. Rob says it's no big deal—pot should be legalized and skateboarding is not a crime. Eileen doesn't agree with her son, but she keeps everything to herself. She's embarrassed to tell, afraid others will judge her family or shun them altogether.

A long, long nightmare—that's what Rob's problems feel like to me. Sure, they're his problem, but I've been so embarrassed over them. I know deep down he's not evil—he doesn't hurt people or rob little old ladies—but the whole situation is something I don't wish to share with others. I haven't even been able to tell my own mother.

I used to fear that I'd turn out to be one of those single moms with troubled boys. Well, it happened. My mother isn't supportive, claiming that kids who do drugs or ride skateboards are rotten. She's just misinformed, but it hurts. And I remember being that way once too.

When Rob was only six he wanted to make friends with an older boy on our street. I remember feeling so protective of my little guy, checking out neighborhood rumors about the older kid. I found out the boy had a poor home life and was considered a troublemaker. I forbade Rob to play with him. Through the years I always made sure Rob steered clear of "bad boys." Now my own son is the kid other moms want their boys to avoid.

Rob's behavior embarrasses me, but at the same time I still love him. It's so hard when other parents brag about their kids. If I say anything about Rob, it's usually about his personality rather than his accomplishments. To say more than "Rob's a great kid" is to leave myself open to prying questions.

And in many ways, my son *is* a great kid. He's gifted in art and draws amazing pictures. He's polite and articulate. He reads constantly. I can look into his gorgeous green eyes and fall in love again the way I did when he was born. It's just that he's got this problem with pot and alcohol—things some people don't understand.

The first time Rob was hauled in for MIP (minor in possession), I was tempted to call everyone I knew. I was scared and angry. The arresting officer gave me a hug and tried to assure me that I'd survive this—she had teenagers too. As soon as Rob was released, I felt so alone and isolated, but I couldn't bring myself to call anyone. I was afraid I'd just hear all my friends and family telling me how to fix Rob.

That's another reason I don't talk about Rob's problems: I want to avoid unsolicited advice. I've heard of other mothers' spilling family problems and later regretting it. One woman said, "In Bible study I shared about our granddaughter's teen pregnancy, and suddenly everyone was an expert." She said she became overwhelmed by so much advice when all she wanted was prayer.

Later on, this same woman discovered that she and her grand-daughter were the main topics at a church social. She hadn't intended for her granddaughter's plight to be broadcast all over the church, but without thinking, people just naturally talked about it.

So I don't put Rob's name on the prayer chain. It's hard enough to deal with this stuff without wading through a ton of unsolicited feedback. People may mean well, but they don't always appreciate another's situation.

And what about Rob? If I tell about his trials with the law, will others forgive him? Or will they draw permanent conclusions about his nature even if he begins to change? There's an old adage about never saying negative things about your spouse to your mom. Later, when you've forgiven your husband, your mom will still think he's a bum because of what he did.

I feel the same way about Rob. Yes, he's got problems, and he should take responsibility for them. He needs help for his substance abuse, and he ought to rethink his attitudes on pot and skateboarding on private property. But in the meantime, he's my son and I love him. I will allow him to take whatever consequences come his way. But I won't complain about him to my mom or my best friend or the prayer group at church. I'm afraid that if I do, they may still think of my son as a criminal long after he's clean and sober.

At the same time, I long to be able to cry on someone's shoul-der—someone who's going through the same thing. For me, the twelve-step approach has helped me open up without fear. Rob and I are attending AA and Al-Anon meetings. It's a great way to gain sup-port without judgment or too much advice. Rob has fallen off the wagon a few times, but he keeps trying. And slowly I'm learning not to feel as ashamed of our situation.

The only other place I take the family skeleton is to my own prayer closet. I might get better results with everyone I know saying a prayer, but this is how I feel comfortable. When I'm upset and sad and hopeless, I know Jesus has a secret place where he'll meet me any time of the day or night.

———

It is difficult to make a man miserable while he feels worthy of himself and claims kindred to the great God who made him.

ABRAHAM LINCOLN

My Shame

MELODY

I turn away and move past her
pretending I must get there faster
I rush down the produce aisle
and ignore a hopeful smile

but what could conversation gain
except to reveal hidden pain
and things I can't begin to share
with someone I feel sure won't care

her son goes out for basketball
she's never been to juvi hall
she doesn't check her baby's breath
she doesn't fear an early death

and yet there's something in her eye
she ducks her head as I pass by
do I imagine what I see
does her expression look like me?

Heartstrings

A MOTHER'S PRAYER

L ord,
I know it will happen again soon—maybe even today. A friend
will pull out photos of her perfect children. She'll want to swap stories
of how her kids are making a mark in the world—for their families,
for themselves, for you, God...

How I dread those moments! Another string on the instrument
of my heart will snap. The music will fade.

Be with me in those times, I pray. Be my strength and hope. As
your beloved child, may I rise above my own feelings of awkwardness,
embarrassment, shame, resentment, or anger. Grant me strength and
grace to share another parent's joy and celebrate your faithfulness.

Thank you for your promise that when my heart condemns me,
I can rest in your presence because I belong to you, and you know
everything, and you are greater than my heart.

Amen.

Section Seven

AM I A PARENT OR THE POLICE?

HEATHER

When Noah was in junior high and still adamant that he'd never consider smoking dope, he came home one afternoon and told me about a mom who'd attended his school that day. She was there with her son to "baby-sit him" since, as she announced to each class, "he can't manage to stay out of trouble with pot, so he has to have his mommy follow him around."

Noah was horrified. I thought she was a genius. I told Noah with some delight that I'd do the same thing if I ever found out he'd smoked pot.

He didn't doubt me at all. And he assured me, sincerely, that he had absolutely no plans to do drugs. Drugs were dumb, he said.

I believed him. And he believed himself.

But of course he did smoke pot. And then he did it again. And again. And I never went to school with him and mortified him the way I'd promised.

You could say we both let each other down. Or you could say that we both had a change of plans.

Noah's new plan in light of teenage wisdom: He'll party "smartly" through college. He'll sow his wild oats but still get good grades. And then he'll grow out of it. "It's not like I'm going to be a grownup and doing all that stuff, Mom. I won't be a loser. I'll stop then."

Noah, like a lot of kids he knows, has come to see the drug scene as just a natural part of teen and young adult life. Part of his duty to society almost. For his parents to want or expect something different is to be unrealistic and unreasonable and thwart life's natural course.

But that, in some ways, is our assignment as parents, isn't it? To be an obstacle, a big boulder in the middle of the wrong road. My working philosophy and plan was always, Baby-sit your child if you have to. And make sure the consequences for doing the wrong thing are so bad that it just isn't worth it.

What I didn't count on was the twisted logic of teen drug users: They are so convinced they won't ever get caught, so sure of their skill at sneaking, that the consequences never enter their mind. And should they get caught, they figure they'll learn from it and get even smarter about hiding what they're doing.

There's another big problem for parents who feel they've been forced to become police: Discipline options at this age are extremely limited and often impractical, not to mention marginally effective. For example, you can take away his driving privileges (and have to drive him to school, to work, to his friends, to the store…yada-yada…yourselves). You can ground him (and hire a private eye to watch him whenever you're gone or asleep). You can remove him from sports teams, the band, or whatever other activity he enjoys (thus giving him more free time to pursue less productive or healthy activities). Or, in short, you can find some other way to make his life miserable (which in turn is guaranteed to make your life miserable).

Yes, it is as much of a setup as it sounds. And the whole time we're administering consequences, the teenager imagines that we are the problem—not dope or alcohol, not the gang or guns or whatever it is that's got our boy lost in its grasp.

No wonder some parents give up, look the other way, and just hope for the best.

But rarely does "the best" follow. And so most of us reach instead for advice, for help, for some definitive answers to the impossible question of how to discipline a son who is often bigger than us, not to mention louder and stronger. This has led to the concept of "tough love"—severe consequences and ultimatums—becoming more and more popular among parents of teens. There's even a support group online for parents who practice tough love. And the reason for that is obvious, I think. Parents need someone to be tough with them in order for them to be tough enough to be tough on their teens.

Sometimes it's about that confusing, isn't it? How do I help my son, love my son, and at the same time refuse to help him when he's in trouble? For example, if I don't bail him out of jail, what if he gets comfortable there and makes even worse friends and falls under even worse influences? Or how can we kick our son out of our home, knowing he has nowhere to go that's good? One mom I spoke to said, "Give him a pup tent, a sleeping bag, fifty dollars, and a nice jacket to use for job interviews."

This kind of extreme measure makes sense in some cases, but I know few moms who could bear to do it. And that's the real problem. Somewhere along the line we have to figure out which is worse: the possibility that we're enabling our son's downward spiral by helping him too much, or the possibility that our lack of help and tangible support in the name of tough love will further alienate him from us and our values, making our love in the end very tough to feel.

Ultimately every parent of a lost boy must answer the question, What is my role in this mess?

My new plan for combining parenting with police work is still in progress. I've yet to discover an airtight answer that's suitable for any and every family. I've yet to come up with one that keeps the teen out of trouble and simultaneously keeps the parent happy and liked by the teen. The only advice I can honestly give that always applies is this: Do what you honestly think is best for your son in the long run.

So I continue with the old plan and a few adjustments. I choose not to baby-sit my grown son. But I do let Noah know that I love him, that I worry about him, and that for his own good, as long as he lives under my roof, there will be rules and consequences.

And you know what? I think Noah is banking on my plan. He still works against me at almost every turn. But deep down, I think he's hoping that his mother will never give up completely. He's counting on me to oppose him every step of the way—if it's the wrong way—as long as I can.

It's not a job any mom likes. Or a part she necessarily plays well. Sometimes we moms cave. Sometimes we're genuinely confused. Sometimes it hurts so much to hurt our sons through discipline or lack of rescue that we wonder who's punished more—them or us. It'd be so much easier to bail on the police part of parenting.

When I feel that way, I remind myself that even God disciplines those he loves. Be it in the form of a fish's belly, a storm, or a talking donkey, God was always willing to be that big ugly obstacle, to stand in the way when a son or daughter was taking a road to nowhere.

God probably hates that part of being a parent too. But love won't let him look the other way. And regardless of what approach to parenting we favor, love won't let us turn away from our lost boys either.

——————

Our children give us the opportunities to become the parents we always wished we'd had.

LOUISE HART

Good Cop, Bad Cop

Janice knows other parents who use the "good cop, bad cop" approach to child rearing. She's a single mom raising three children, so she has to play both the "good" and the "bad" cop. When Janice's middle son, fourteen-year-old Trent, assaulted her one night, she realized the situation was too big for her to handle alone. She called the police and had Trent arrested.

I've been on my own since my youngest was just a baby—their dad isn't in the picture at all. Sara graduates from high school this year, Trent is fifteen, and Mark, my baby, is a third grader. It hasn't been easy to raise three kids by myself, but I've learned to ask for help from friends, my church, and the community.

Things went pretty well until Trent hit adolescence. He'd been an average kid, into sports—he especially loved baseball. He did all right in school until seventh grade. That's when Trent started to become a handful, both at home and at school. I started to get complaints from his teachers about his behavior. He was getting into fights almost every day. I grounded him and took away his allowance, but he didn't seem to care.

He began to talk back at home, too, and argued with his brother and sister almost constantly. Everything bothered him. If anyone touched his things or asked him a question he didn't like, he'd explode. He was especially protective about his room and seemed paranoid about all of us "going through his stuff."

I began to suspect he was experimenting with drugs, so I hauled him in for an evaluation. His drug tests came out inconclusive, so I thought I couldn't order him into treatment. But over the next few months his attitude got even worse.

By eighth grade Trent was out of control. He wouldn't listen to me anymore and refused to attend church with the rest of the family. He spent as much time away from home as he could. One night he came in late, and I confronted him about where he'd been and what he'd been doing. We stood in the kitchen at three in the morning, arguing. Trent's face turned red, and he got this crazed look in his eyes. He screamed at me to leave him alone, cursed at me, and when I refused to back down, he slapped me. He threatened to hit me again if I didn't back off. By that time, Sara and Mark were up and watching us with wide, frightened eyes.

I remember Sara's pink p.j.'s, how the little angels printed on them looked so innocent in that horrible situation. I realized I couldn't let the violence go on. I yelled to Sara to take Mark into the bedroom—and to call 911.

Three officers arrived and had to wrestle Trent to the floor. He kicked and tried to spit on the cops as they cuffed him. They arrested my son for assault and menacing and also found some pot in his pocket. I cried when I saw Trent in shackles and handcuffs, but I knew I had to let him go. He spent the night in the juvenile detention center and later had to face a judge, pay fines, and go on a year's probation.

I had a harsh awakening that night. I finally saw how drugs can turn an otherwise good kid into one who sleeps too much, spends all his money on dope, and fights to the point of violence with his mother and siblings. The signs had been there, but it took me a long time to do anything so drastic. I knew when I decided to call the police that Trent would probably hate me, but I was determined to stop the craziness. He didn't speak to me for two months, but deep down I knew he would love me again.

Trent didn't change right away. He tried to beat the system by taking niacin to alter his UA's (urinalyses), but he got caught and had to start over. He ran away for two weeks because he didn't want to follow my house rules. When he came back, I saw how much I had changed too. I insisted that Trent agree to stay clean and follow the rules before he was allowed to move back in. I think that's really what "tough love" is about—taking a stand and then not budging.

My parenting skills are better now, and I've learned that yelling doesn't work. Oh sure, we still have arguments—what family doesn't? But I no longer give up when my children push my buttons. I rely on my church a lot—for everything from men who are willing to get involved with my boys to moral support in my small group when things are difficult. And Trent knows that if he behaves as he did that night, I'll call the police again.

I wish there had been some other way. I prayed for strength as they hauled my boy away. But I couldn't be afraid anymore to take control of my child's life when he was a danger to himself and to the family.

Trent is still working his program. He's had ups and downs, but he's making progress. We're learning how to talk to each other again, and he says he's stopped hating me. It's amazing: When I drew the line and Trent knew I was serious, he began to improve. And as I become more consistent as a parent, Trent gets easier to be around. With God's help we're making it past the tough part of tough love.

A Prodigal Prayer

GIGI GRAHAM TCHIVIDJIAN

I sit and wait…wondering.
My child is late.
And my mother's heart is worried.

All is quiet…all is still.
All but my anxious heart.
And as my eyes fill up and spill the tears
Upon my upturned face,
I ask,
"Lord give me grace."

…

Lord bring him back.
Please bring him back into this land again.
But while he is away
With him closely stay.
And bring peace to my troubled heart.
Let the tears that start
Each day to flow
Be turned into a prayer
Because I do not know
What to do…

Where to start!
Lord please take a worried mother's heart
As an offering today
And bring my boy home to stay.

(Based on Jeremiah 31:10-20)

=======

The age of puberty is a crisis...
It is the passage from the Unconscious to the Conscious;
from the sleep of the Passions to their rage;
from careless receiving to cunning providing.

RALPH WALDO EMERSON

So Much Potential

Cindy and Rick couldn't figure out their son, Paul. Teachers and friends in high school called him "brilliant...charming...sure to succeed," and yet after graduation, Paul seemed to flounder. His parents tried everything and finally threw their hands up in despair.

Paul was always a handful as a child, and yet everyone seemed to like him. And even though he got into various scrapes during his grade-school years, it seemed he could charm his way out of almost anything. But Paul really came into his own in high school. Involved in almost every activity, he knew everyone and everyone knew him. Although his full schedule sometimes frustrated us, we were proud of him. We enjoyed his school plays and musical programs. And he brought a lot of fun and color into our lives. Paul was the kind of kid who was the life of every party.

After he graduated from high school, we had no cause for concern. Or so we thought. Because of his less-than-brilliant grades, we all agreed his first year of college would be better spent closer to home at the local community college. And Paul seemed okay with this. He decided to move out with friends, and even though we thought he was a bit young for that, we didn't hold him back.

But what followed really threw us for a loop. Paul grew increasingly reckless and irresponsible. It started out with things like unpaid traffic tickets and not showing up at court. His fines quickly piled up. And then he began to indulge in alcohol, and not just a beer or two. He occasionally became so intoxicated that his friends feared for his life. And then he'd borrow money from his friends (who were growing scarcer all the time), but he never paid them back. His bills continued to pile up. It was plain to see he was in way over his head.

Rick and I didn't know what to do. We felt responsible for his bad behavior—like his problems were our problems or maybe even our fault. We tried to get tough with him, acting like his probation officers and keeping track of his every move. Not that it did any good. And over and over we'd "explain" things to him—I guess it was more like lecturing. Then we'd help him out of his scrapes, give him money for fines or whatever. But after a while we realized that Paul was getting himself into these fixes and Paul needed to get himself out.

The hardest thing I've ever done as a mom was to simply step back and watch my son make a perfect mess of his life. Looking back I realize it was only a couple of years, but at the time it seemed like it would go on forever. I wondered what had become of that kid with all the potential.

Finally, after giving up the pursuit of a degree in his third year of college (which we begged him to reconsider), Paul got a pretty good job and quickly (due to his charm and wits) moved up into a fairly decent management position. Slowly he began to pay off his bills and began living like a semiresponsible human being. His dad and I both sighed in relief. But after only six months, Paul decided to abandon that dependable job and go off to do something completely different. It seemed unbelievably crazy, unreasonably risky, and totally ridiculous. We jumped right back into our parental position and adamantly warned him against this choice. We begged and pleaded with him to listen to reason and to rethink this senseless move. Why couldn't he stick with what seemed safe and secure and turn down this foolish job opportunity?

But Paul assured us that he knew exactly what he was doing. We sadly watched as he shoved the last of his belongings into his jam-packed little car. Then we both hugged him and told him that we loved him no matter what happened, and sadly we waved good-bye, expecting the worst. Would our son never learn? Off Paul went on a thousand-mile trek, in a car about to fall apart, to take this crazy job in Los Angeles.

Well, as it turned out, this time Paul was right and we were wrong. That crazy little job has led from one exciting opportunity to the next. Paul has been places and done things we never dreamed he would do. And now, a dozen years later, Paul is happily married, with children, and a great success. He has a well-paying top management position in a first-rate company. And our relationship with him is better than ever.

It's hard to believe how badly he floundered during his early college years—how we almost gave up hope. Paul still remembers the day we told him we'd love him no matter what. He's told us that the way we stood by him through thick and thin has helped him more than we'll ever know. It just goes to show that you can never tell what lies around the next corner for your kids, but if you do your best and allow them to make (and deal with) their own mistakes, things usually work out in the end.

Train up a child in the way he should go,
And when he is old he will not depart from it.

PROVERBS 22:6

Give Me This Soul

ANONYMOUS

Lord, give me this soul!
I have waked for it when I should have slept.
I have yearned over it, and I have wept,
'Til in my own mind the thought of it held sway
All through the night and day.

Lord, give me this soul!
If I might only lift its broken strands,
To lay them gently in thy loving hands—
If I might know it had found peace in thee,
What rest, what peace to me!

Thou wilt give me this soul!
Else why the joy, the grief, the doubt, the pain
The thought perpetual, the one refrain,
The ceaseless longing that upon thy breast
The tempest-tossed may rest?
Dear Lord, give me this soul!

Waiting for the Harvest

A MOTHER'S PRAYER

L oving Father,
Strengthen me today to guide and discipline my children, even when what's right feels all wrong. (Seems to me like "tough love" is toughest on moms!) When my parenting abilities are pushed to the limit, grant me the clear-minded wisdom that comes from above—spiritual insight that starts with the fear of God and a trust in your unfailing goodness. Take away the fog of emotions, confusion, doubt, harsh judgment, and self-condemnation. Help me to make smart, practical decisions under pressure.

By your great power and love, bring other positive influences to bear on my son—authorities, counselors, employers, laws, natural consequences, other relatives, and friends. Most of all, fulfill your promise that loving discipline—no matter how painful at the moment—will bring the kind of inner change for my son that will result in "a harvest of righteousness and peace" (Hebrews 12:11, NIV).

Amen.

WHEN HE HITS BOTTOM—AGAIN

MELODY

When your son's blown it a few times—okay, let's say a lot of times—don't you start to wonder how low he can go? I mean, what does it take to get the message across? How many times must he be sickened by his errant behavior? How many fines does it take before he'll realize the law is here to stay? How many lost jobs, lost friendships, broken promises, broken hearts does it take before he gets smart and figures it out?

My son Luke says he likes learning from his mistakes. And that's great, I tell him; we should all learn from our mistakes. But how many mistakes do you need to make before you learn the lesson? How many times must you hit bottom before you realize it's no fun down there? And believe me, Luke's hit bottom more than once. But somehow he always manages to climb out, dust himself off, and move on. He stays on track for a while, but eventually, within two or three months, he takes the plunge again.

As Luke was closing in on twenty, we really started wondering if this pattern in his behavior was something more than just rebellious adolescence or the terrible teens. Because of his on-again-off-again problems with substance abuse, we suspected he might actually be trying to "self-treat" for some kind of chemical imbalance. By then we were discovering that a number of people (on both sides of our families) suffered from various chemical imbalances—everything from ADD (attention deficit disorder) to OCD (obsessive compulsive disorder) to schizophrenia to bipolar disorder (manic depression). We could've become the poster family for some national mental health magazine.

We decided to arrange a complete psychiatric evaluation for our son. At first the doctors suspected ADD because a lot of Luke's behaviors seemed to fit that diagnosis. I could see hope in Luke's eyes and a sense of relief that we might finally be discovering the answer. And yet after trying several types of ADD medication, it seemed clear that it wasn't really helping. As a result, Luke became even more frustrated. He began to withdraw into himself, almost as if he were giving up. He began to sleep more, and he couldn't hold down a regular job. He might say he wanted to go to college and find work, but somehow he just couldn't get himself from point A to point B and actually do it. While he wasn't in any sort of serious trouble anymore—he wasn't using drugs, hadn't been arrested, didn't have any unpaid fines, and had pretty much given up "partying"—he seemed lower than ever before. He appeared to be hitting another sort of bottom—rock bottom, we feared. But we didn't know what to do.

About this same time, we learned that a close relative (one whose behavior we had often compared with Luke's) had been diagnosed with bipolar disorder and been put on lithium. He had now been stabilized for several months. Well, it wasn't the first case of bipolar disorder in our family, so I began to read up on manic depression. And presto, it suddenly started to make sense. It seemed quite possible that Luke suffered from this same disorder.

So I talked with Luke, showing him a list of the symptoms and a general description of the disorder. He immediately identified with almost everything he saw. The diagnosis seemed to fit. His older brother, now majoring in psychology in college, felt it was likely too. But the best part was the relief in Luke's eyes—like maybe there was a real reason for his behavior all along and maybe he wasn't just an irresponsible fool.

Later on, I told Luke's psychiatrist how I felt guilty, even stupid, for not suspecting manic depression a lot sooner. I mean, the writing had to have been on the wall for years—it seems so completely obvious now. But the psychiatrist said it's always tricky even for professionals to accurately diagnose adolescents with any kind of chemical imbalance because teens are well known for their ups and downs, highs and lows. As a result, it's hard to know what's normal and what's not for an individual teen. Sometimes it takes hitting rock bottom before anyone can begin to figure these things out.

I guess the good thing about rock bottom is that there's only one way out—and that's to go up. Luke's on his way.

———

A stumble may prevent a fall.

THOMAS FULLER

Talent to Waste

Eveyln is a single mom who lives in Chicago with her son, Virgil. She thinks Virgil isn't doing that bad, when you consider he doesn't have a father and he lives in a "hard" neighborhood. However, Virgil has repeatedly been caught with drugs. Here Evelyn shares her hopes for Virgil, as well as the story of what she considers her worst day yet.

Have you ever noticed how some kids just seem to have the talent not only for doing stupid things but also for getting caught doing them? That's my son, Virgil. When he uses what you call poor judgment, he does it with poor judgment. Other kids—I could name five or six of my son's friends I know of for sure—smoke dope and do crack all the time and would never be so dumb as to get caught. But Virgil has been in trouble because of drugs about ten times now.

Maybe the best place to start to tell you about my Virgil is with the worst day in our history. Every parent has one of those stories. When I'm talking to my friends, we can all describe a "worst day" or a time when we thought our son had hit bottom. But then lots of times it turns out that that wasn't the bottom at all! Maybe a son goes to prison. Or one of his homies gets shot. Sometimes *that's* not even the bottom. Isn't it funny how we sometimes spend as much time hoping our lost boys will hit bottom as we do hoping they'll straighten up and fly right?

Actually, I'm one of the luckier moms I know around here. (We live in the part of Chicago where Oprah doesn't go.) My Virgil is smart, and at least he's still in school. As far as I know, he's not in a gang, although he looks like he's in one. Anyway, Virgil has a talent besides getting caught when he's doing dumb things. He plays the saxophone, and he's been playing in the school jazz band for the past two years. He's really good at it. This band is one that lots of kids want to get into. The best part is that Virgil and his band teacher get on really well. I guess you might call the teacher a mentor for my son, which is what he needs since he doesn't have a daddy.

Every year there's a competition between the high schools. The jazz bands all play for each other and for a jury of judges, and if they win, it can help them get scholarships and stuff. So last week Virgil went on the bus with the whole band to a competition an hour away. His band was supposed to play in the afternoon, but they let the kids loose for lunch, and my Virgil decided to be stupid. He got some pot and—get this—some vanilla extract. I never knew it, but I guess the stuff contains lots of alcohol. So Virgil and his buddy went to five different stores buying bottles of the stuff.

He and his friend went into the bathroom at McDonald's and started doing the dope and drinking the vanilla. Well, of course, some man came into the rest room while they were in there and smelled the stuff. He reported them to the manager, who called the cops. The boys ended up getting arrested, right there at McDonald's. The cops cuffed them both, right in front of everyone eating their lunch, and put them in the police car. They called the school where the competition was happening to tell the band teacher that his sax player and drummer had been arrested. Well, the teacher was so upset. And I can understand why. He thought Virgil had learned his lesson about drugs from the other times he'd been caught. He's got big hopes for Virgil.

Sadly, the whole band couldn't play in the competition because they were missing two key musicians. So all the kids were mad at Virgil too, of course. And I had to go down to the police station to get him. I was fuming.

When I got there, though, I could tell my son had been crying. I'd never seen Virgil so upset. My tough-talking boy, crying! I couldn't believe my eyes.

He got suspended from school for two weeks. He hasn't faced the court yet. But the worst part for him has already happened: He let all those people down. I think he got so used to thinking that doing drugs was just about him—his choice, no one else's business, and all that. Now he finally sees that it wrecks things for lots of other people too. He's been real depressed since then, moping around here like his dog died. But I think the truth is getting through. He says he dreads going back to school. He thinks everybody in the band hates him now.

His teacher came by to talk to Virgil. He wants him to stay in the band. I was so relieved to hear that. The teacher is hoping, and I'm hoping, and even Virgil, I think, is hoping to God that this is finally the bottom—at least as far as his getting into trouble with drugs. If it's not the bottom, I don't think I want to be there when he does hit bottom.

But I know I will be. Because that's what mamas do: hit the bottom with their kids over and over and keep loving them. I'm praying that in the end that's going to make all the difference. Just my being here and saying, "Virgil, you have something to waste. You have a talent. Don't be a fool."

***

It is never too late to be what you might have been.

GEORGE ELIOT

He Is Risen

Leah and Richard Green tried for years to conceive a child. They adopted a daughter, Jen, who was full-blooded Native American. A few years later Andrew arrived as a tow-headed toddler, taken from his crack-addicted biological mother. The Greens loved both their adopted children and considered it a ministry to help unwanted kids. Jen was always a handful but managed to graduate from high school and chose to return to her family on the reservation. Andrew, at fifteen, was quiet and easygoing—until he discovered the power of alcohol.

The only thing that has seen me through these past few years has been the assurance that God won't give us more than we can handle. And believe me, some days I'm not so sure about that. Five years ago on the night before Easter, I wondered if God had given up on us altogether.

Andrew was a "crack" baby, but he wasn't as fussy or hyper as some kids born to drug addicts. He had the biggest blue eyes, a great smile, and hair like straw. Rich and I fell in love with him instantly, just as we had with his older sister, Jen.

We took special parenting classes when the kids were small, hoping to minimize some of the struggles that can come with adopting kids who missed out on bonding with their first caregivers. In spite of our best efforts, however, Jen struggled in school, and in her teen years she got into drugs and ran away a lot.

When Jen announced that she wanted to go live with "her people," as she said, with the Yaqui, we were heartbroken. We let her go and then tried to concentrate on Andy.

Things went all right for a while—Andy got involved in Cub Scouts and even earned his Arrow of Light badge. He moved up to Boy Scouts. We made sure he was connected to the youth group at our church, and we tried to do things as a family. Andy's grades as a freshman were only average, but he didn't have behavior problems at school. Overall he was doing well.

Then in January of that year we got some horrible news. Our daughter had been found dead in Los Angeles of a heroin overdose. We had no idea she wasn't on the reservation anymore. Because of the seven-year age difference between Jen and Andy, they hadn't been real close—so we didn't think it was strange when Andy didn't seem too upset over the news. But after the funeral, he spent most of his time in his room or away from home. He had some new friends, ones who thought church was stupid and boring. His grades got worse, and he slept a lot. We tried to get him to go to counseling, but he stomped out of the room any time we mentioned it. "Leave me alone!" became his mantra.

Rich and I were so frustrated. We already felt guilty about Jen's death. Now what would we do to help Andy? I placed his name on as many prayer chains and lists as I could contact, and Rich and I both fasted and prayed for our son. Nothing helped.

The night before Easter we were all going to attend a church supper. At the last minute, of course, Andy refused to come along. I wanted to scream at him to get into the car. Instead, I slammed the door of his bedroom, and we left without him.

I kept thinking about the scripture, "In your anger do not sin: Do not let the sun go down while you are still angry" (Ephesians 4:26, NIV). I couldn't stop thinking about Andy and wanted to apologize. We left the supper early because I was so upset by the incident.

Back at home, Andy was nowhere to be found. I called a couple of his buddies, but no one knew where he was. Then the phone rang.

It was a neighbor who lived on the next street. She was an acquaintance, but we weren't close. "My husband and I found your son face down in our front yard," she continued, "and he's barely breathing. It looks like he's had a lot to drink."

Rich and I rushed over, and there was Andy, barely conscious, on the wet ground. The neighbor had rolled him onto his side so he wouldn't choke on his vomit. A tall vodka bottle lay nearby. It was nearly empty.

We were so scared we could barely think. Rich and I laid Andy on the backseat of our car. I was so stunned that the neighbor had to instruct me to ride back there with him while Rich drove to the emergency room. All the way there I cried and prayed and held my precious son's head while he vomited again and again.

The ER nurses said it was touch and go that night. Andy's blood alcohol was high enough to kill. Stomach pumps and charcoal and the grace of God eventually saved his life, but it took hours to stabilize him. By morning he was released, and we took him home.

Easter had a very special meaning for me that year. Christ had risen, and so had my son. I sent the neighbors an Easter lily to thank them for their part in saving Andy.

Some days I still feel it's all too much and that I just can't take any more. But when Andy says he's hit bottom this time and is really ready to start over, maybe God is telling me he'll handle it when I am too weak. My son has been spared twice. I'm praying that will be enough.

I Feel So Alone

Sheryl's kids have been central in her life for almost twenty years now. A stay-at-home mom, she volunteered at their school, taught Vacation Bible School every summer, and was basically "always there for them." She never anticipated that anything would go wrong—why should it?

I thought God had smiled down on us by giving us the perfect family. Tim and I couldn't have been happier with Scott and Lisa. And unlike the way we were raised (in broken and dysfunctional homes), our kids, we determined, would fare much better. I chose to stay at home so we could do all those fun things like Scouts and sports and baking cookies.

Just as our kids hit their teens, Tim and I were asked to help with the youth group at church. We asked Scott and Lisa how they felt about this, and they thought it was great. To them it simply meant more camps and retreats and parties. And so we became involved in this ministry. For a while everything was going great. I can even remember telling other parents that parenting teens was nothing—a breeze even. "Just keep those communication doors open," I would say with a bright smile.

Then Scott turned sixteen. And suddenly everything changed. He started saying that church and youth group were dumb and that he no longer wanted to go with us. We tried forcing him at first and then realized it only made him hate it more. Besides, how did it look when the youth leaders' son (who didn't want to be there) sat in the corner and sulked? We talked to our pastor about quitting the youth ministry, but he encouraged us to hang in there. He said we were doing a good job and that Scott was probably just going through a little teen rebellion. So we stayed on.

Tim seemed to take it all in stride. He said we needed to let our son make these decisions for himself. "We came to our faith on our own without help from our parents," he reminded me one evening after a long argument I'd just had with Scott. I knew what Tim said was true, but I wasn't sure. I was afraid Scott was getting involved with the wrong crowd—that he'd do something really bad—and then what would I do? As a result of my fear and shame, I found myself closing up to people. When they'd ask about Scott, I'd just brush off their questions and redirect the conversation. And soon I began to feel very alone.

It wasn't long before I discovered that Scott was smoking pot. I found a bong and a partially full baggie in his backpack one morning before school. (Yes, I admit I'm a snoop!) Tim had already gone to work, and I wasn't sure what to do. But I knew I couldn't let Scott out the door without talking to him.

I can still remember how Lisa watched in horror as I cornered Scott. Within minutes my "confrontation" was out of control. Loud, angry accusations flew back and forth. Scott was furious that I'd gone through his bag. And I was livid that he was dabbling in drugs and carrying stuff like that around with him—even to school! "What if you get caught?" I demanded. "Who do you think will bail you out?" Of course, he was certain he'd never get caught, and if he did, he'd never call his uptight parents to help him out. And then he swooped up his pack and stomped out the door.

I called Tim's office, crying hysterically. And as usual, Tim remained calm. He seemed to have all the "right" answers but nothing that made me feel better. "We just need to talk to him," Tim said. "He needs to know we love him but that we can't accept this kind of behavior." *Yeah, yeah,* I thought, *I'd rather just lock him in his room and do homeschool until he turns twenty-one.* But when Tim came home that evening, he had a plan to talk to Scott. And when Scott finally came home (after ten), the three of us sat down and talked. To my surprise, Scott seemed sincerely sorry. He agreed to everything Tim said, and, like magic, it seemed our nightmare was over.

Until a few days later when we got a call from the police. Scott and a friend had been picked up at the mall and charged with possession of marijuana. I hung up the phone and blew up at Tim—as if this were all his fault. Tim didn't respond and simply put on his jacket and went to the police station to pick up Scott. And once again we got the full apology and "I'll never do that again…" from Scott. Tim believed our son. I did not. But I kept my thoughts to myself. Unable to even pray, I cried myself to sleep that night.

For days I just closed myself off—from Scott, from Tim, from Lisa, even from God. Looking back now, I can see I was depressed and probably should have sought help. But at the time, I was too lonely and miserable to do anything. I even made up excuses not to go to church or work with the youth group. But somehow, like the Energizer Bunny, Tim just kept on going and going. And Scott, although he seemed to straighten out for a week or two following the arrest, slowly began to slip back into his old ways: blown curfews, signs of substance abuse, slipping grades. And all the while Tim calmly handled everything. He even began to deal with things without telling me. And I began to resent him more than ever.

Lisa, observing her brother's mistakes, seemed to grow up overnight. It's as if she were trying to become perfect to make up for Scott's screwups. And in the meantime, I felt like a powder keg, just letting everything pile up inside of me, not talking to anyone, and fearing that the next phone call would be the police telling me my son was in more serious trouble.

Finally I just totally fell apart, cried nonstop for days—until Tim finally talked to our pastor and was advised to get me in for some professional help. I suppose my breakdown was something of a wake-up call for everyone. After I'd received some treatment (counseling and antidepressants), we all decided to go in for family counseling. Yes, even Scott.

I can't say our troubles are all behind us now. I still get panicky when the phone rings at night, fearing it might be Scott in some kind of trouble again. But I've reopened my prayer lines. And I do think we're making real progress as a family. It seems like Scott is honestly trying to change this time.

In some ways I think my hitting bottom brought Scott back to reality. Not that I want him to feel guilty for my problems (okay, maybe a little), but I think God used my breakdown as a wake-up call for my son. It would be great if he could learn his lesson without having to hit rock bottom too.

Be anxious for nothing,
but in everything by prayer and supplication, with thanksgiving,
let your requests be made known to God;
and the peace of God,
which surpasses all understanding,
will guard your hearts and minds through Christ Jesus.

PHILIPPIANS 4:6-7

Just One Gun

When Lisa met her husband, Bob, she knew he was a big gun fan. She asked him to keep his arsenal at a buddy's house, and he agreed. But after their home was burglarized, Bob insisted on bringing home one gun. After they had a son, Lisa insisted that Bob hide this gun under lock and key. Years later their son, Jack, discovered Bob's hiding place. What happened next would change two families' lives forever.

It happened five years ago, but it's still hard to talk about. And when I do, it's so painful it feels as if it all happened yesterday.

I guess I should begin with the gun. My husband, Bob, has always loved guns, and he's been a member of the NRA since he was a teenager. He knows I hate them, and for a while after we were married, I wouldn't let him keep any in the house. So he kept them over at his friend Sonny's house. Now and then they'd go hunting or target shooting for fun. That was fine with me.

Then we were robbed. We came home from a week's vacation at the beach to find our house half empty. Burglars had taken the television, the stereo, the CD collection, all my jewelry, and even some of our smaller pieces of expensive furniture.

Bob put his foot down and brought home just one of the guns. It was a revolver, a .45 magnum. Reluctantly I went along but made him promise to keep the weapon safely hidden since by then we had a five-year-old son, Jack.

The gun was never a problem, and I didn't even know where Bob kept it hidden. I didn't *want* to know. Maybe that was a mistake. Maybe if I'd known where it was, I would have hidden it even better than Bob did. But as it was, I forgot all about it, and years and years passed without our ever needing to use it.

By the time Jack was a sophomore in high school, we could see that he was going to have troubles—or give us troubles, you might say. He kept skipping school, and he started hanging out with a crowd that looked rough to me. He didn't attend church or youth group (which he said he hated and wouldn't be forced into). Little did we know that someday we'd long for "troubles" this simple.

There were no real signs leading up to what happened. It was a school day like any other. Jack darted out the door that morning with his backpack when his friend Tom, who had a license already, pulled up in his jacked-up Ford truck. Tom and his younger brother, Milo, who was seven, had been giving Jack a ride all year. They always dropped Milo off first at the elementary school.

Unbeknown to me or my husband, Jack had discovered the key to the lock box in which Bob kept his gun hidden. That morning when Jack left the house, he had the gun in his backpack, wrapped in a dishtowel from our kitchen. I still remember how surreal it seemed to me when five hours later a police officer showed Bob and me the gun in a plastic evidence bag, along with my favorite red-striped dishtowel.

I got the news in a phone call from the school secretary, a woman I often joked with when I took in Jack's forgotten lunch or a book he'd left behind. The story that unfolded over the next few hours was this…

Jack was excited to show his friends the gun and knew that Milo, being so little, would be even more impressed than his peers. He'd been careful to make sure there weren't any bullets loaded in the gun, but he didn't understand how a gun can look empty while harboring a bullet in the chamber. Later I felt guilty about how I had refused to let Bob introduce Jack to guns. If Jack had learned some basic gun safety, maybe this whole thing wouldn't have happened.

In the truck, for a joke, Jack whipped the gun out of his backpack, turned sideways, and aimed it at Milo. Milo was in awe, fascinated. He begged to hold the gun, and Jack let him. When Milo gave it back, Jack playfully put the gun against Milo's temple and fired. The sound of the gun and the screams that followed alerted neighbors to phone the police. But, of course, Milo had died, very visibly, the moment Jack pulled that trigger.

Today Jack is in juvenile jail, and he will likely remain in some kind of jail until he's twenty-five. But the real jail, the prison of his guilt, I don't think he'll ever escape. Not that regret is making him a better person, however. He's meeting all kinds of sordid people in jail, and I don't think he'll come out of there okay in the head or in the heart. I don't know what to do about this. I just pray and pray for him.

A lot of moms think they've got trouble with their boys because they won't clean their room and they get C's on their report cards. They have no idea, is all I can say. No idea at all.

I think that's why I hang on to the hope of heaven more than most people. I have to. When your life here on earth has become so tragic and painful, and there's not much hope in sight, you put a lot of stock into heaven, where we'll all be healed and whole. Finally. I hope.

A Prayer for
Marilyn Manson

MELODY

I've seen your music, your lyrics, your CD covers, your
    biography.
I've recognized your violence, your hatred, your
    cruelty to yourself.
I've looked upon your abhorrence of God.
All littered like refuse across the floor of my son's
    bedroom.
And it's frightened me.

But I know that your name is really Brian.
And that you, too, are a mother's son.
And while I cannot stand what you do,
I can care about you,
Just as your loving father, God, cares about you,
And even loves you.

And so I pray for you, Brian.
I pray that God will gather you up into his arms
And love you like you've never been loved before!
I pray that your self-blinded eyes will be opened

And you'll see how precious you are to your Father
   God
And receive all that he longs to give you.

I pray that you'll look in the mirror
And see yourself for who you really are:
A lost and lonely, broken little boy
Who is loved completely by the One
Who was beaten, ridiculed, and executed
So that you might run with abandon
Into your Father's arms.
I pray that you will.

Amen.

In the Ditch

D ear God,
I know you love my son, you'll never give up on him, and you
have a good and meaningful life in mind for him. But sometimes I
see another truth altogether: a young man in the ditch, run off the
road again by his own foolish insistence on pursuing sin and selfish-
ness at any cost.

You know my anguish so well, God. How many times you saw
your beloved children, Israel, in the same ditch, despite your constant
love!

When my son hits bottom again, when I feel all alone with my
grief, when I've used up my friends, when I've run out of believable
cover-ups, when my life mocks me and my son's behavior is a disgrace
to you—oh, be Savior and Friend to me! And most of all, be Lord
and Redeemer for my son.

Thank you that your compassions are new every morning and
your faithfulness is unending.

Amen.

I WANT TO TRUST GOD, BUT...

HEATHER

S ometimes it's hard for us to imagine that God loves our sons in the same way we do. After all, he's got this whole universe to run. At times he seems distant and impersonal. How and why would he take special care of our kids?

Recently my son Noah was asked to write an essay about his problems with pot for an Internet site where my husband and I write a regular column. His story was very honest (even I learned some things), and in response I received e-mails from many other parents who had kids in similar straits.

One of them was from a mother I'll call Mary. She wrote to tell me about her own teenage son, Kyle. He was a good kid, got great grades, played every sport, had always been well loved. Like other Christian mothers, Mary prayed for her son, for his safety, for his happiness. Then one night Kyle smoked pot with some friends and was killed in a related car accident. It had only been a few months since her son's death, and her grief was still raw. She begged me to tell Noah, "It's not worth it!"

Her message of caution was sincere. But behind her words, I thought I could hear something else. Painful questions. Questions like, "Why is my son dead while yours is still getting second chances?" and "I prayed too. I trusted God with him. Why did God let me down?"

We hear it, and we say it so often to each other: *Trust God with your son. Trust God!*

But can we *really?*

What happens when our prayers go unanswered? What happens when we, like Mary, trust God with our son, pray for him passionately, and then the positive changes we hope for don't happen—or worse, something tragic does?

Granted, there are many inspiring stories of answered prayer, mothers who believed and prayed for years and saw their lost children come "home." But if we imagine that trusting God guarantees that our kids will be kept safe in their cars when they drink and drive, or that they will not suffer the consequences of being in a violent gang—then, *no.* On some level we can't trust God. Or at least we can't trust God in the way we'd like—a way that works like a life-insurance policy and protects us and our kids from any and all harm regardless of human behavior.

We can only trust God in a much bigger way. A way that considers our time on earth a short stay before heaven. A way that acknowledges that our children belong to God first, and he loves them most. Ultimately we can't put our trust in what God will *do* but in who God *is.*

Once, as I wrestled with this issue of trust concerning Noah, I found myself saying to God, "But you were never a mother!"

And he answered in my spirit, "Yes, I was!"

It's true. God has a mother's heart. In many ways the entire Bible is God's "lost boys" story. God had children and he loved them desperately, but they went astray and hurt themselves and broke his heart. Ever since, he's been trying to bring them back home.

Imagine this scene with me. A mother sits in a rocking chair with her baby son in her arms. As she ponders his future, she is suddenly overwhelmed with fear. She's keenly aware that she is fallible. She knows she will make mistakes as a mother. She feels helpless to protect her son from tragedies and accidents she can't foresee. Good grief, she can't even control the rain that beats against her son's window! She wishes she could see—and control—the future. She wishes... At that moment she is reminded of the perfect, all-powerful, all-loving God of the universe. She clutches her precious bundle closer to her chest and asks herself, *Can I trust him?*

Now imagine God's holding close his own perfect, beloved Son to his bosom. He looks down at his children on earth and asks himself, *Can I trust them with my Son?*

He sees that they're sinful, warring, filled with hatred and jealousies. He imagines the worst, which he knows is what's to come. They will kill his Son in the most humiliating, unbearable way. They will flog and crucify him. They will make Jesus suffer, bleed, and cry out for his Daddy to save him. But God will not rescue him from the inevitable consequences of human sin.

No. God cannot trust them with his Son. Of this, God is certain. But he is equally certain that there is no other way to bring them, his prodigal world, back into his arms. "O Jerusalem, Jerusalem, you who kill the prophets and stone those sent to you, how often I have longed to gather your children together, as a hen gathers her chicks under her wings, but you were not willing!" (Luke 13:34, NIV).

And so, with anguish in his mother's heart, he offers up his beloved Son to save the sinful world.

And the frightened new mother rocks her baby and wonders of God, *Can I trust him?*

You see the irony. But the real challenge is to take this message to heart: *We can and should trust God with our sons.* Because he is a Father. Because he is a mother at heart. And because we would be foolish not to hand over those we love most to a God who loves them even more.

———————

But Zion said, "The LORD has forsaken me,
And my Lord has forgotten me."
"Can a woman forget her nursing child,
And not have compassion on the son of her womb?
Surely they may forget,
Yet I will not forget you."

ISAIAH 49:14-15

The Other Shoe

When it comes to Zachary, Rhonda's seventeen-year-old, she realizes she's in constant fear, waiting for the other shoe to drop. His angry outbursts are unpredictable, and the whole family feels the effects of his temper. Can Rhonda trust God to keep them all safe?

When the middle-school teacher suggested that my son needed help for his anger problem, Zac thought it was a joke. He went to anger management classes because he was forced, but he still found reasons to explode on the whole family. My husband, Hal, and I have tried different ways to help him, but our oldest son acts like he's just mad at the world.

I know Zac might sound like a monster, but he's a really sweet kid with thoughtful gray eyes and red hair like Hal's. When he was little he brought stray animals home and was always very sensitive and kind. He'd cry if he accidentally squashed a bug! But as he got older his temper began to flare red hot in an instant.

Hal's a Vietnam vet—he was given a lot of medals for bravery. When our sons were little, Zac and Sean played war like a lot of boys do. It was hard to tell them not to when their dad had been in a war. But after I started a day-care business in order to stay home with them, I removed all toy guns from the house—I didn't want the kids playing violent games. Zac would build guns from LEGOs or shoot with his index finger. No matter how I tried to stop him, he always wanted to blow away all the imaginary bad guys.

When Zac was twelve, his teacher called to say our son drew horrible scenes of war and killing all over his papers at school. Every picture showed blood and gore, and his teacher was concerned about Zac's preoccupation with violence. This was before the school shootings like Columbine in 1999, so we thought Zac simply had a vivid imagination.

Zachary doesn't have a lot of friends, but he isn't a total loner either. I'll admit he's drawn to other boys who are interested in violent movies and games. Whenever I've forbade Zac to hang out with these kids, he's thrown outrageous fits. He just seems so lost and lonely. I've prayed for an answer, but frankly I've found myself becoming afraid of my own son.

After the teacher warned us about Zac's drawings in school, we took our son to a counselor. The counselor told us Zac was a very angry boy, but we couldn't understand why. We weren't divorced or alcoholics. We went to church as a family. Hal took an active part in the boys' upbringing. But Zac's eruptions were becoming more frequent and more violent.

He took a lot of his anger out on me. The counselor said, "Maybe Zac knows you can't stop loving him, so he feels safe venting on you." It was true that I could never stop loving Zac, but we were all walking on eggshells at home, waiting for the next scene. Being challenged in any way really sets Zac off. If we say no or disagree with him—even about trivial things—he often yells and screams. Twice in the past year he's raised his hand, but thank goodness he never hit me.

Sean has had trouble with his older brother's outbursts too. One day Zac thought Sean had taken one of his compact discs. The two of them got into an argument over it. They yelled at each other, and then Zac started shoving Sean. A lot of brothers fight, but Zac got a wild look in his eyes. "If you ever touch my stuff again, I'll kill you," he said. Sean told me he was scared his brother might really mean it.

Zac usually feels terrible about his behavior when he isn't in one of his "moods." After threatening his little brother in such a menacing way, Zac admitted that he has a problem with anger, and he says he's ready to deal with it. So all of us are in family counseling, and Zac is participating willingly this time. I've learned in our sessions that I don't have to sit by and take his anger. I can be assertive and not allow Zac to control me. If he gets violent or menaces any of us, Hal and I have agreed to call the police. The more Zac knows we'll stand up to him, the less likely he is to use rage to get his way.

Zac is changing too. He's learning to take responsibility for his anger, and he's practicing techniques for keeping himself under control. He's seeing that he doesn't have to be perfect, but he does have to treat others with respect.

I'm learning that I can trust God without being a doormat. It's not easy, but I'm setting boundaries and refusing to play Zac's game. Humor helps—it's almost impossible to get angry while you're laughing.

For me, trusting God doesn't mean I can just sit back and see what happens. Zac and I are both learning to be assertive instead of passive or aggressive. Today trusting God means I'm not afraid of my son anymore. I'm handling things differently instead of just waiting for the other shoe to drop. And all the while, I'm relying on God to give me the daily wisdom and courage I need.

Have courage for the great sorrows of life
and patience for the small ones;
and when you have laboriously accomplished your daily task,
go to sleep in peace.
God is awake.

VICTOR HUGO

Nine Hundred Reasons to Trust

Amanda and Ned's sixteen-year-old, Wes, is a model student and is work-ing toward the rank of Eagle Scout. He's never been a troublemaker. While his parents have struggled to keep their daughter off drugs and in school, Wes has quietly been the "good son." That's why Amanda was so shocked one day when she opened the family's monthly phone bill.

I nearly fainted. Instead of the usual minor charges for long-distance calls, the bill said we owed almost three thousand dollars. *Three thousand dollars!* When I showed the bill to Ned, he said, "There must be some mistake." I wish that had been the case.

I contacted the phone company immediately and learned the awful truth: For the past month someone in our home had repeatedly called a 900 number, racking up charges to a sex hot line. The tele-phone representative patiently explained how these hot lines advertise in magazines, promising free calls. What the ads don't say is that once the caller dials the free number, the call is switched to another line, where the fees can run over three dollars per minute. I felt stunned and sickened at the same time.

My husband and I have always tried to be open and honest about things—including sex. Even though the kids take health classes in school, Ned and I have talked to both kids about how we view sex as a beautiful part of married life. We thought we'd done a good job. We'd told them about abstinence before marriage, mutual respect, even STDs and birth-control methods. Ned and I both encouraged our kids to ask a lot of questions.

When the 900-number incident happened, I suspected Wes was responsible. Just a few weeks earlier I'd found a dog-eared *Playboy* magazine under his bed. When Wes claimed it belonged to a friend, my son's freckled cheeks had turned a deep red. He threw the magazine away without objection and said he wouldn't bring home any more of them. Ned and I chalked it up to a boy's natural curiosity. But now, having to ask my son if he'd made calls to a pornographic hot line was one of the most difficult things I've ever had to do.

I had all afternoon to think about how to approach Wes. I was convinced he wouldn't knowingly run up a huge bill he knew we'd see. Yet I was embarrassed and angry about the incident. If our son had made these calls, then he'd violated our trust—and it hurt. I bowed my head and cried, tears splashing across the phone bill.

I didn't want to explode all over Wes when he got home, but I couldn't ignore the situation either. What was the correct way to handle this? I was afraid I'd say the wrong thing and drive Wes to do worse things. As I prayed for answers I felt an inner nudge. *Trust me,* God seemed to say. *Just trust me.*

After school Wes burst through the door and slung his backpack on the table. He piled cookies on a plate, poured a big glass of milk, and plopped down across from where I sat. I smiled at him, wiped tears and mascara from my eyes, and picked up the soggy statement.

"What's wrong, Mom?"

I handed him the bill. "We got this in the mail today," I said. "What do you know about it?"

My son's jaw dropped open as he studied the amount due. "Three thousand bucks! How could we owe this much money?"

I explained where the charges came from. "The phone company says these calls were to hot lines—sex hot lines." I felt my own cheeks burn.

Wes stared at the numbers and then at the floor. For a long time he said nothing. When he looked at me again there were tears in his brown eyes.

"The ad said it was free," he said.

As the story unfolded, I was amazed at how calm I remained. Wes's friend—the one with the magazine—had shown him an ad that promised free calls to "sex kittens." On several occasions the two of them had waited until after midnight, then dialed the hot lines. As I'd suspected, the boys were unaware of the true cost of the calls.

I didn't yell at Wes. I told him to think about what he'd done. After a time he apologized and offered to get a job to pay off the huge bill. He said he would never engage in this activity again. I breathed a sigh of relief.

On a one-time-only basis the phone company waived the charges because Wes was a minor. Still, Ned and I handed Wes consequences for his actions. For a month his allowance went toward the normal telephone bill, and he won't be getting the cell phone he wanted for his birthday. I believe Wes when he says he won't do this again, but we had blocks installed on our line to keep him from being tempted to make long-distance calls without permission.

Wes says he's learned that trust is a fragile thing; once it's been damaged, it takes a long time to heal. The fact that he owned up to his actions means a lot, but he understands that he'll have to earn back our full confidence.

I'm learning more about trusting too, even if it's through circumstances that I'd rather not face. As my boy grows up, God nudges me more often, saying, "Trust me," when I doubt things will work out. I'm learning to trust those nudges.

Why, God?

Gwyn's life has been anything but easy. A family history of mental illness plagues her as well as her husband, Ron, and unfortunately their two children haven't been exempt. Gwyn says it's only by the grace of God that she and her husband have managed to stay together through it all and ride out the worst storms.

My husband and I have mental illness and substance abuse on both sides of our families, so I don't know why we were surprised to discover our children suffer from these as well. But when we got married nearly twenty-five years ago, we were idealistic, fundamentalist Christians. And we honestly believed that if we raised our children in a certain way, God would make everything work out "right." Now, I'm not blaming God for all our troubles. But I'm hoping that someday I'll get to ask him some pretty tough questions— face to face. In the meantime I'm learning I just have to trust him with these things.

I suspected something was wrong with our daughter, Sarah, when she was a baby. She never made eye contact or bonded in the way I thought babies should. Being in a fundamentalist church, we took her to be prayed for again and again. But nothing ever seemed to change. We sought professional help when Sarah turned ten, and she was diagnosed as a sociopath. She's been in and out of various treatments and hospitals ever since.

But we always thought Jacob was our "normal" child. I mean, it seemed impossible that we could have two children with severe problems. As a result we probably focused all our hopes and dreams on our son—an unfair burden for any child to bear. Sometimes I still feel guilty, like our high expectations were what caused Jacob's life to spin out of control. But his psychiatrist says Jacob was just like a time bomb waiting to go off. There was nothing we could do to stop it.

Throughout his first fourteen years, Jacob seemed like your typical kid. Involved in sports and activities, he was loving and kind and had a great sense of humor. Honestly, he felt like a gift from God. But something started to change right around age fifteen going on sixteen. He became moody and withdrawn. He'd spend hours in his room after school, just drawing or writing or listening to music. At first we were concerned, but after talking to a counselor friend, we were assured it was just typical adolescent behavior. The counselor said Jacob probably just needed space and that we may have been smothering him with our love—possibly to make up for what was going on with his sister.

For a while Jacob seemed to improve. He began going out more and spending time with friends. And he seemed happier sometimes. He'd have his good days and bad days. The good was really great, but the bad was pretty scary. It was confusing. Just when we'd get really worried about Jacob, he'd suddenly straighten up, find a part-time job, act responsibly, and have a good attitude. We felt as if we were on an emotional roller coaster.

And we weren't too sure about his "friends" either. They all seemed to have some sort of chip on their shoulders. By the end of his sophomore year, we discovered that Jacob and his friends were experimenting with drugs and alcohol. Devastated, we begged Jacob to see a counselor. But by then he'd decided that all psychological and medical professionals were "quacks" (he'd probably seen too much while we dealt with his sister).

In the beginning of his junior year, Jacob was caught with pot and kicked out of school. In desperation we actually moved to a nearby town and enrolled our son in a new school, thinking he just needed a fresh start. But within weeks he'd managed to hook up with a similar crowd, and the same problems continued. Now the only difference was that my husband had a two-hour commute every day!

Then one night we got a phone call from a frightened friend, saying that Jacob was unconscious and needed medical attention. We called for an ambulance and met him at the hospital to find out from his buddy that Jacob had "taken some pills and washed them down with a fifth of vodka." After hours of grueling stomach pumping and other emergency treatments, Jacob recovered. His father and I sat by his bed, held his hand, and told him we loved him. Then I asked, "Why did you do this?" thinking he'd say he was just looking for fun. "I didn't want to live anymore," he said, his eyes focused on the IV tube sticking out of his arm.

Jacob finally agreed to see a psychiatrist and was diagnosed as bipolar (manic-depressive). When we read the description of this illness and its symptoms, we knew it must be true. Besides, my aunt was manic-depressive. And Ron's deceased father was an alcoholic who exhibited the same symptoms. We've had to become educated about how these illnesses run in families.

My first reaction after Jacob was diagnosed was to question God. *How could he do this to us—twice?* Why didn't he answer our many prayers to heal our children? And why is there mental illness at all? But, of course, these are the questions without any answers.

The good news is that Jacob's medication is working. Well, mostly. It's still a constant balancing act to keep him somewhat stabilized, but Jacob is cooperating with his treatment. Once he realized he had an illness, he accepted it, and now he's really working with his psychiatrist and a Christian counselor toward a healthier life.

As far as my unanswered questions go…well, I finally decided that all I can do is believe that God knows what he's doing. All I can do is trust him for the many things I don't understand and hope that someday it'll all make sense. In the meantime we're just thankful that Jacob is alive. And we still pray for medical breakthroughs for both our children.

My Two Sons

MELODY

My two sons,
I always wanted you.
Even when I was a little girl
Playing with baby dolls.
I clothed them and fed them,
Rocked them and sang a lullaby,
Thinking that one day
I would have babes of my own.

And God gave me you,
My two sons.
And I clothed you and fed you.
I rocked you to sleep
And sang you a lullaby,
And it was wonderful.
I wanted it to last
Forever.

But quickly you grew older,
With sturdy legs and grinning faces.
And we made a sandbox,
Played with LEGOs,
And read stories.

We learned to ride bikes,
And mended owies.
And you grew up.

Now you are young men,
Both over six feet tall,
With whiskers.
It feels like you don't need me—
Very much.
And I have to let go
And trust God to care for you,
But it's the hardest thing I've ever done.

My two sons,
I always wanted you.
But now all I can do
Is watch and pray
That you will let God
Clothe you and feed you,
Rock you and sing you a lullaby.
And it will be wonderful.

Saving Love

A Mother's Prayer

L ord of all your lost children,
Some days nothing changes for the better, no matter how hard I
pray and hope and long for a miracle. But I trust you anyway, God,
because I believe you are always at work.

Some days I wonder why I still follow you when you can't or
won't seem to rescue my wayward son. But I trust you anyway, God,
because I know you love him enough to honor his choices while you
tenaciously work to redeem his life.

Some days I stop feeling any trust in you. But I will trust you anyway, God, because you are truer than my feelings and more faithful
than my heart and stronger than my son's rebellion.

Some days the worst does happen. But I trust you anyway, God,
because the worst doesn't change what's true. Jesus came to endure
and die for the worst, and nothing on earth—even the worst—is
beyond the reach of his saving love.

Amen.

Part III

WHAT WILL

BE...

I'LL ALWAYS LOVE
MY LOST BOY

HEATHER

T he apostle John once declared that "there is no fear in love" and "perfect love casts out fear." I'm sure in principle he's right. But he was never the mother of a teenage boy.

I fear so many things for Noah. I fear the physical dangers of the drugs he dabbles with. I fear that this phase of his life will lead to an addiction, a lifelong way of coping that will cost him dearly. I fear that my son doesn't understand the power of drugs, the weakness of his own heart. I fear death. I fear tragic accidents in which he'll be wounded or wound others. I fear, above all, for his happiness and for his spiritual safety.

And if I'm honest, I fear having to love him "in spite of."

I've met those moms. Moms who have to accept that their son is a coke addict who won't get help, or that he's in prison, or that he's practically ruined his life with his poor choices. Moms who must embrace a son in spite of her worst fears coming true.

I fear this so much that I tell myself, *There's still hope. And time. My son could still turn out just like I want him to.*

And then I realize, with some shame, that taken to the next step, what I really fear is having to deliver on that unconditional promise I made to my son over and over while he was growing up. You know the one. How many times have we all said it? "Mommy will always love you no matter what you do. There's nothing you can do to make Mommy not love you."

Did we mean it? And if we did, what exactly did we mean by it?

When Noah was little, he'd try hard to think of something that could make me not love him. Maybe the whole concept just didn't correlate to anything he'd learned, at least not from cartoons.

"Even if I robbed a bank?" he'd ask, his blue eyes wide.

"Yes, honey, even then," I'd answer.

"Even if… What if I set the house on fire?"

"Yes, honey, even then."

A few years back I met a man who understood the fear of loving "in spite of." I met him at a writers' conference. He'd lost his wife to cancer a year before, so I figured he wanted to write about his marriage. But as it turned out, his motivation for a book about "love that loves no matter what" was his drug-addicted son.

Years earlier this handsome silver-haired father had tried everything to save his son. The boy went in and out of rehab. He spent time in prison. Nothing seemed to work. Finally the son simply gave up and settled into the life of a "functional" addict.

Disappointed and disgusted, the father gradually alienated his son. They never spoke. The son knew not to call until he was clean.

And then, at some point after his wife died, this dad realized that years were passing, that time was wasting. And he missed his son. "I wanted to spend time with him, know him, eat dinner out with him, go fishing or to movies."

Laying aside his judgment, his disgust, his urge to shame, and his bitter disappointment, he told his son, "This is who you are, how you are. I'm done trying to fix you. I love you. I miss you so much. Let's enjoy each other, even if it means that sometimes when I'm with you, you will be on drugs."

So they golfed. Walked the beach. Attended concerts—this conservative white-haired widowed dad and his drug-addicted son.

As far as I know, the son is still battling a cocaine habit. But the dad's story helped me see how easy it is, without meaning to, to place invisible limits on love. Limits based on "values." Limits based on what we so badly want someone else to be. Limits based on our own fears.

For some of us it's too early to know to what reaches our unconditional love will be challenged. Our worst fears could still come true. In the meantime our lost boys are still asking, "Even if...? What if I...? Still...?"

And perfect love says, in spite of fear, "Yes, honey. Even if..."

===

To wait an Hour—is long—
If Love be just beyond—
To wait Eternity—is short—
If Love reward the end—

EMILY DICKINSON

Stubborn Love

She is the wife of a prominent pastor in a large church, but nothing pre-pared Ellen for what happened when things began to go off course for their teenaged son, Caleb. And although she didn't agree with her hus-band's position, she chose to stand by him. And yet she somehow managed to stand by her estranged son as well.

I hate to say it, but Caleb was always my difficult child. And yet he was my only son, and I loved him dearly—fiercely even. At first we attributed his difficulties to his high IQ and strong will. But as he progressed in school, we began to realize that something else was going on as well. Hardly a week passed without some sort of problem arising. We tried to take these incidents in stride, working closely with Caleb and the school. We tried to encourage him in his areas of interest: art and drama. And we could see his skills in these areas were very advanced—even if we didn't always appreciate his subject matter or direction.

We hoped he'd outgrow his behavior problems eventually. But as Caleb approached his middle-school years, we decided to get a psy-chological evaluation. He was diagnosed with ADD/ADHD (atten-tion deficit and hyperactive disorder) and put on Ritalin. It seemed to help a little, but getting him to stay consistent in taking his medica-tion was a challenge during those years. And troubles continued. By high school he began to abuse his prescribed medication as well as dabble in other drugs. Looking back, I think it was a form of self-treatment. Caleb didn't feel well and was looking for something—anything—to make him feel better.

During this time my husband, Ken, was busier than ever pastoring a rapidly growing church. And I know that Caleb's behavior (and now strange wardrobe) were a source of irritation and humiliation for Ken. To put it mildly, our family was a little stressed out. And we worried about Caleb's influence on his younger sister. We didn't want her to follow in her brother's footsteps. But we could see that even as Caleb seemed to be constantly self-destructing, he still had a good heart and a sweet spirit. To me he just seemed lost. It frustrated me deeply that nothing seemed to get through to him. Not his father's stern lectures, not my loving help, not even God. And he became progressively suspicious of doctors and psychiatrists. Soon he refused to see anyone. He also became a vegetarian, and mealtimes in our home turned into something of a three-ring circus.

At the end of his junior year, Caleb was placed on academic probation. We suspected his drug use was increasing, and he'd been arrested a number of times for strange things like reckless endangerment or trespassing. Finally Ken reached the end of his patience. He told Caleb to shape up or ship out. And Caleb left.

Well, I thought it was just a show. But when Caleb didn't return the next day, I became worried. On the third day he called, telling me he'd moved in with friends. I begged him to come back home, promising that we'd work this out, smooth things over. But then he asked what his dad thought about that. And I couldn't lie. Ken had made his position clear: Caleb could come home only if he agreed to comply with our rules, get clean, and return to school. Caleb said he wouldn't make promises he couldn't keep.

My heart was broken. I was torn in two. I came before God again and again, down on my knees, praying through my tears. But nothing changed. Ken didn't back down. Caleb didn't come home. Finally I found out where Caleb was living and went to visit. It was obvious that he and his friends had been smoking pot and doing who knows what else, but I just calmly sat down on a sagging red plush sofa and talked to my son. I told him that no matter what, I loved him. And I told him that God loved him even more. I told him I'd always be there for him and asked if there was anything I could do to help. Then I hugged him and went home.

I returned the next day with a bag of groceries, careful to purchase only vegetarian items. It wasn't easy to go to that place, but my brief visits with Caleb continued, and I think our relationship was strengthened. Even when I noticed signs that some of his roommates were possibly bisexual or homosexual, I kept my thoughts and judgments to myself. To be honest, I'm not even sure about Caleb's sexual orientation anymore. But why should anything surprise me now?

I'd like to say that Caleb outgrew this phase and returned home. But he never did. It's been ten years now, and he's still living in pretty much the same conditions. He has a job at a restaurant, but he also pursues art and drama in his spare time. He dresses more strangely than ever, sometimes even cross-dressing. And he still claims he doesn't believe in God. But every time I see him, I hug him and tell him how much I love him. No matter how many parts of his body are pierced or what kind of clothing he chooses to wear, I will always love him—unconditionally and forever.

Children need love,
especially when they do not deserve it.

HAROLD S. HUBERT

Without a Conscience

When Pamela and Mark adopted Matthew at age seven, they felt certain things would go well. But as the years passed, the problems mounted. And they weren't ordinary problems. Matthew's violent temper was shocking, and he seemed incapable of grasping any basic sense of right and wrong. Pamela feared she was raising a psychopath. And now she fears she was not that far off...

Matthew charmed us from the very first day. Teachers and dormitory staff of the residential school for kids with disabilities where he stayed during the week told us of serious behavior problems, but we thought they just didn't know how to handle him. Except for a surprising tantrum (which we attributed to fatigue) toward the end of Christmas vacation, his behavior with us was exemplary.

We couldn't have loved the cute, funny kid more, and we eagerly looked forward to bringing him home each weekend. But during the long summer vacation Matt began to show his true personality. He would lie, deliberately hurt our other children or get them into trouble, and become violently angry whenever we limited or disciplined him.

Gary, one of our other kids, had poorly controlled epilepsy. Sometimes when we weren't watching, Matt would tease Gary enough to get him upset, then take and destroy one of his favorite toys before his eyes, and usually that would bring on a seizure. Matt admitted that he caused the seizures deliberately because it was interesting to see if he could. At times he would do it to distract attention from his own misbehavior.

Any time he didn't get what he wanted, Matt would fly into a rage. Often he would pick up a broomstick or a chair and smash a window or hit one of the other children with it.

Once he stole a hundred dollars from my purse, sneaked away from school during the lunch recess, and spent all the money on baseball cards at the corner store. His teacher called us when she discovered him giving the cards away by the dozens.

Matt showed no remorse for stealing. Instead he insisted he had just as much right to spend the money for what he wanted as I did. He had used it to try to buy the friendship of his fellow students. With his charm, Matthew could make friends very quickly with children he had just met, but after a week or so of being deceived, manipulated, and physically hurt, they would want nothing more to do with him. Most of the time he was on his own.

We knew that Matt had come from a difficult background, and we tried our best to teach him the difference between right and wrong while helping him feel loved and secure. We transferred him to the special education class in a local school so he could live at home. We got professional counseling for him and consistently used the most respected methods of behavior management. And we prayed a lot. Surely it would be just a matter of time until he straightened out! There were still plenty of times when he would turn on his charm and convince us that we were succeeding, sometimes for weeks at a time.

It wasn't until he had lived with us for a couple of years and we had become completely emotionally attached that we realized how serious Matthew's problems really were. He used his charm to manipulate people but didn't seem able to care about anyone except in terms of whether or not they gave him what he wanted. To him the difference between right and wrong was a matter of arbitrary preference on the part of whoever had the most power. If he was likely to be punished for doing something, it was wrong; otherwise it was okay.

He couldn't seem to understand the basic concept of truth and falsehood either. One Sunday our pastor corrected himself during a sermon by saying, "I made a mistake. What I should have said was…" Matthew turned to me, jutted out his chin, and declared loudly, "See? Even the pastor tells lies!" My heart ached as I realized that my son still just didn't "get it" in spite of all our efforts. His inability to comprehend basic moral principles was almost like just another of his learning disabilities.

Years later I read a description of what psychopathic killers were like in childhood, and it fit our beloved son to a T. True to form, Matt became so dangerous when he reached his teen years that we finally decided giving him up might be the only way to protect our other children from serious injury or worse. We agonized over the choice. Even though it broke our hearts to do so, we finally told Matt he had to leave our home.

We have heard from Matthew only occasionally in the years

since he left us, always when he wanted something. Because he won't keep in touch or let us know how to reach him, it's been impossible to maintain ties. We do know that he's been in and out of jail numerous times, and now there's a restraining order preventing him from contact with his former girlfriend and their children (whom we have never met) because of his abusive behavior. I wish I could see Matthew and find out how he's really doing, but frankly, I wouldn't want him showing up on our doorstep. He's just too dangerous.

I still pray daily for Matthew and for the protection of the people involved in his life. And even though sometimes I feel embarrassed to say it to certain people, I still love Matthew with all my heart. I used to wonder about mothers whose sons killed people or robbed banks and ended up in jail or worse. How could they still love this "monster"? When they claimed to, did they really mean it?

Now I understand completely. And in a way, my love for my lost boy is a gift. Nothing has helped me more to understand just how powerful and unrelenting God's love must be for Matthew and for moms like me.

But God, who is rich in mercy,
because of His great love with which He loved us,
even when we were dead in trespasses,
made us alive together with Christ
(by grace you have been saved),
and raised us up together,
and made us sit together
in the heavenly places in Christ Jesus.

EPHESIANS 2:4-6

Forever Ours

Bill and Theresa Martin raised their family while Bill was in the army, moving from post to post as their five children grew up. After Bill's retirement from the military, the Martins settled in a small town in Washington and joined a local church. One by one the kids left home, starting families of their own. Bill and Theresa looked forward to travel and other activities as soon as the "nest" became empty. But their youngest sons got entangled with methamphetamines, and now the Martins never leave home for long.

B ill and I thought we'd be relaxing by now, enjoying retirement and our grandchildren. But much of the time we're still parenting our two youngest sons, who have been in and out of drug rehab for years. I love my sons, but things are very difficult at times. Both "boys" are over twenty-five years old, yet they always seem to be starting over.

I've heard of other grown kids who live with mom and dad briefly while they save money or if they lose a job. I believe in helping my family during difficulties, but Bill Jr. and Nick have each come back home more times than I can count. I'm beginning to wonder if my sons will ever leave home for good.

When we moved to this town in Washington, we didn't know that along with beautiful rolling hills and a mild climate, the area was known for its "meth" users. Methamphetamine, or speed, is a huge problem here, and both my sons got sucked in. The drug is cheap and very addictive. It's been called the poor man's heroin for the way it hooks people and ruins lives. Bill Jr. and Nick are proof that speed does kill—if not the body, then certainly a person's hopes and dreams.

It's so sad because both Bill and Nick are talented in many ways. Bill is a terrific artist, and Nick has an outgoing personality and a fantastic smile. Bill has struggled with drugs and alcohol for most of his adult life—substance abuse runs in our family. He's tried to kick his habit several times and has been successful for periods but often relapses. His younger brother served in the navy after high school, and I didn't think he'd end up using. But drugs got to Nick, too.

In some ways Bill Sr. blames himself for the boys' problems. My husband quit drinking twenty years ago but still feels responsible for passing on the substance-abuse gene. I think heredity plays a part, but there is a solution to addiction. Recovery is a tough road, but I believe it's available to anyone who really wants it.

At one point we felt we couldn't tolerate the boys' drug use another second. But we couldn't accept our kids being homeless either. Rather than let them move back into our home, Bill Sr. built a large storage shed in the backyard. He insulated the walls, installed carpet, and let the boys sleep inside. We call it the Homeless Shelter. One or the other of the boys has lived there ever since, sometimes for months.

Other times we've watched our guys get motivated and find jobs or go into rehab. They strike out on their own, and I think, *At last they're getting their act together.* Unfortunately, the progress never seems to be permanent.

A few years ago Nick started attending NA (Narcotics Anonymous). He met a fellow recovering addict there, fell in love with her,
and decided to marry. We threw a big church wedding for them.
Nick had a job, a car, and soon a son. I was thrilled. But when Nick
injured his back at work, everything began to unravel. The marriage
got into trouble, and before we knew it, Nick and his wife and baby
had moved into our backyard shelter. We suspected both Nick and
his wife had resumed using drugs. Eventually the two of them split
up, and while Nick continues to wait for his worker's compensation
case to be resolved, he's living in the Homeless Shelter.

Bill Jr. has a similar story. His wife has a mental illness, so whenever they fight or Bill gets fired from a job or spends all his money on
drugs, he comes "home" to the shelter. My husband and I are afraid
that years of drug abuse have impaired our son's ability to think
clearly. I'm heartbroken to see him and Nick have so many problems.

When we must travel, we worry about our belongings. Drugs
make people do things they probably wouldn't do if they were clean.
On several occasions valuables have gone missing. I hate the idea of
my own kids stealing things from us, but I also realize how desperate
the need for drugs can be. I deal with it by no longer giving them an
opportunity—we get someone to stay at the house whenever we
must be away.

The situation has gone on so long that I wonder how my lost
boys will manage after we're gone. We're in our sixties, after all. I keep
praying my sons will find their way out of the hole they've dug, but
I'm afraid for them both. The only thing that keeps me from losing
hope entirely is my faith and the support of our little congregation.
At church I can sit in the pew and cry if I need to. My prayer group

has a standing order to pray for Bill Jr. and Nick. And our pastor keeps Bill Sr. and me busy, helping out with activities and church business. I go to services as often as I can to empty out my problems to God and to refill myself with what I call my heavenly weapons: faith, hope, and love.

I haven't stopped hoping that Bill Jr. and Nick will move out on their own for good and lead successful, prosperous lives. My fears— that the speed will cause even more damage, maybe even kill them— are real, but I don't face them alone. I may have to start over every day, but I'll always love my boys, no matter what.

How Do I Stop?

MELODY

How can I quit loving him?
Can I block this primal maternal instinct that beats
    within my heart?
It would be easier to stop the sun from coming up.
Can I hold back this passionate concern that defies all
    reason?
I could easier hold back the tide.

So how do I avoid this jagged blade
That relentlessly twists in my gut?
How do I suppress my excruciating devotion
So conflicted with resentment,
Where my only reward is more pain?
How can I quit loving my son?
When despite his defiance, his insolence, his outright
    rebellion—
He is heart of my heart, my child, my own.
How can I cease to love him?
It would be as useless as attempting to stop God from
    loving me.

I'm Counting on You

A MOTHER'S PRAYER

Dear heavenly Father,

Thank you that your love for your children doesn't change. Whatever happens, you have only good in mind for us...and you love us always and forever. Thank you that because Christ gave his life for us, we can come to you no matter what kind of week we've had in our family or what shape our heart is in.

That is the kind of love I want for my children. That is the kind of love I want to show them, the kind of love I want them to know is true—always there, always the same, always committed to their best, even when they can't see it and don't believe in it anymore.

By your Spirit, grow that Christlike, lifelong, life-transforming kind of love in my heart today.

Amen.

I'M READY TO LET GO

MELODY

There's something they forgot to mention when we accepted this daunting task of motherhood. Sure, we knew that our babies would be completely dependent on us for their care—24/7. We knew that we'd nurture and protect them, that we'd hold their little hands as we crossed the street. But no one ever mentioned this "letting go" thing. I don't know about you, but letting go of the ones I love most hasn't exactly been one of my mothering strengths.

My sons are twenty-two and going on twenty-one now. Young men, I know. But in my heart, they're still "my little boys." And yet I know I must let them go. I've known that for several years now. Still, I believe that letting go is a process. It begins from the moment they take their first steps or utter their first "no!" It's the healthy separating that must happen between mother and son if our boys are to become independent and experience autonomy. And even though my mind understands all these developmental facts, my heart often betrays me. I still want to grab my boys back to me, hold them, and protect them. But I can't.

Over the past few years I've been letting go progressively, in stages. But I believe it's in the last year that I took the big plunge.

Nothing spectacular happened to bring this realization over me—let's just say it was a "God thing." One night I was praying for my boys, as usual, before going to sleep. And it hit me—kaboom! They are not really *my* boys. I didn't create them. I didn't weave their DNA together. I didn't know them from the beginning of time. No, the truth is they are *God's* boys.

With this fresh realization came a great wave of relief. I thought, *Well, God, if they're your boys, then you ought to be able to take care of them. You ought to be able to make something really great out of their somewhat mixed-up lives. You ought to be able to draw them to yourself and show them who you really are and how much you love them.* Ahh, big sigh…

What a weight was lifted from me that night. Now this has become my regular prayer for my sons: *God, they're yours—you help them, you care for them, you love them!* And it's not as if I'm shirking some motherhood responsibility. Not at all. If anything, this new line of thinking—this prayer—has strengthened me to love my children even more. I no longer feel the need to "do something" to make things better. I can simply love them and let God do what needs doing.

I can honestly say that my relationship with my sons began to improve after this revelation. We get along better now than we ever have, and my love for them has never been stronger or more unconditional. I know they no longer feel stifled or smothered by my love, because now I love them in a way that says: You're free. You have wings. Now go and fly!

My sons live on their own now, and they've amazed me with how mature they're becoming. Oh sure, their apartment isn't the way I'd keep it, and they don't always eat right, but to be honest, they're living more responsibly than they ever did under *my* roof. And they're happier too. When I go to visit them, we actually sit and talk, sometimes for hours (this rarely happened when they lived at home). I think it's all a part of that letting-go thing. Letting go and letting God.

And here's another unexpected benefit: I've found that as I've really let go of my sons and entrusted them to God (who's been their Father since the beginning of time anyway), I have a much calmer spirit. I'm more relaxed, and I worry and fret less. Quite frankly, life is a lot more fun!

I sometimes wonder, *What took me so long?* Why didn't I "get" this sooner? But I realize it was a process and that God was probably gently guiding me to the place where I could truly relinquish my sons and acknowledge that they really do belong to him. I'm sure I'll have to continue reminding myself of this truth, but now I feel confident that even if more trials and problems arise with my sons (and I know they can and likely will), I will be much better equipped to handle them.

Recently it occurred to me that there's another really good thing about where I am now. In one way I've realized that my sons will always be "my boys." Yes, I know they belong to God too. But I will always have those tender memories of my sweet, milky-breathed, bright-eyed babies, their precious first smiles, their boyish pranks, their tender hearts—and all that other good stuff that came with raising my sons. As a mother, these things are mine and mine alone! I've been doubly blessed—I got to enjoy many treasured moments of raising these boys, and yet I can trust God for the final outcome of their lives. Isn't that like having the best of both worlds?

*The last step in parental love
involves the release of the beloved;
the willing cutting of the cord
that would otherwise keep the child
in a state of emotional dependence.*

LEWIS MUMFORD

Let's Play a Game

Sam and Serena have been married for twenty years. They've always prided themselves on having a "happy" home full of laughter and light-hearted fun. But when their son Carl began getting into trouble with marijuana and alcohol, all that changed. Serena was brokenhearted, angry, and frightened. Every time Carl got into trouble, she let him know exactly how upset she was. Her screaming, crying, and hysteria made their point. But they also upset everyone in the family. Were her outbursts really helping Carl? And could Serena learn to let go?

My husband, Sam, and I have always enjoyed doing things with our kids—and they've enjoyed each other. We like to play games together and go skiing together. We laugh a lot, and we've been told that we seem like a happy family.

But lately my son Carl's troubles with pot and booze have changed all that. His rebellious behavior has affected everyone in the family, and now the atmosphere of our home is no longer jovial. My husband and I have had trouble understanding how such a good kid as Carl, who began a personal relationship with Jesus at age five and always loved God with his whole heart, could make such bad choices once he hit adolescence. He's been caught either drinking or doing dope about ten times in the past couple of years, and he's only sixteen.

The first incident involved drinking at an underage party. After my husband and I got over our shock, we grounded Carl. He seemed truly sorry and repentant. Then it happened again—and again. Each time he'd say he didn't want to do it, but he couldn't help it. Each time I became emotional and cried. Then usually I got angry. I'd yell at Carl, "How could you lie to us? I can't believe you did this!" Carl would always say, "Mom, don't take it so personally. It's not about you."

But it is personal. It feels personal when your son is sneaking behind your back, lying outright about where he's been and what he's up to. I think what Carl means when he tells me not to take it personally is, "Mom, I can't stand it when you cry and act so hurt. I feel guilty."

But the fact is, I wanted him to feel guilty. I imagined that knowing how much he hurt his whole family, including his little brother and sister, might help to deter him. So far, it hadn't.

Then one day when Carl had been caught smoking marijuana again, his brother Brennan, age eleven, came to me with his big brown eyes full of tears. "I want to go to Charlie's house to spend the night, Mom. I hate to be around here when it's going to be like this."

It finally hit me. This was ridiculous. Why should our whole family suffer every time Carl decided to be stupid? Yes, Carl needed to encounter consequences. But why should we pay the emotional price for his mistakes? I talked Brennan into staying home and promised it was going to be okay this time.

That night, before dinner, Sam and I confronted Carl with what we knew. This time I didn't yell or cry. It was extremely hard, but I tried to let go of my anger. Sam and I calmly laid out the consequences, and we told Carl we were sorry he was making his life so painful.

After dinner that same night, I suggested that the family play a game together.

"All of us?" Brennan asked, glancing at Carl, then at six-year-old Wendy.

"Yes," I said. "All of us." And, amazingly, we had one of the funnest nights we'd had in a long time.

Carl is still touch and go in his walk with God and his dabbling in drugs. But no longer is our family thrown into despair and turmoil every time he falls. As a result, Carl is coming to realize more fully that the problem is his, not ours. As long as I was reacting so wildly, his focus was on the fact that *Mom is mad again, hurt again.* Now that I am out of the way, Carl is left to face his problem without the buffer of my reactions. I've let go of Carl's problem and, in some ways, of Carl himself. Maybe now my son will be able to hear the voice of God in his ear, instead of just mine.

═══════

Perfection is a road,
not a destination.

BURK HUDSON

Guardian Angel

When Maria found the colored bandana in thirteen-year-old Tomás's room, she hoped he was only a "wannabe," a term she knew kids use to describe others who dress and act like gang members but don't actually belong to a real street gang. She also knew of the pressure many Latino young men face to join gangs. Maria was desperate to rescue her only son before gang life took him away.

From the time he was a tiny baby, I've told Tomás that he will be the one in our family to go to college. He's done great in school and studies really hard. But not long ago I found a blue bandana in his room. My heart nearly stopped because I know gangs use bandanas to show their colors.

Tomás is a good kid, and he's got a lot of support from his family. If there's anything he wants to do, he's got sisters, grandparents, aunts, uncles—we all try to help each other. But here in our neighborhood, our barrio, there's one thing that's really hard: staying out of the gangs.

I am very proud of my Mexican heritage, but in some ways our culture makes it hard for the kids to succeed. Girls are still expected to help care for their younger sisters and brothers and to do a lot of housekeeping chores. And boys, well, boys think they must prove their machismo, often by doing dangerous things. The gangs around here are a big part of this.

To keep Tomás away from gangs, we've been very active in our church. Tomás always enjoyed the youth group and had been chosen last year to be a special youth delegate at a conference for our denomination. But when the day came to attend the conference, Tomás suddenly wanted no part of it. With a sick feeling in my gut, I remembered what our pastor had told us once: When kids get into trouble, church is one of the first things they let go.

That morning I pleaded with Tomás to keep up with church, but he was very rude and disrespectful. In Spanish he snapped, "You're nothing but an old woman!" I was shocked. He had never spoken to me that way! He stomped out and didn't come home until very late.

I couldn't sleep. All night I prayed and cried. My husband, Benicio, tried to comfort me and said he would talk some sense into our son. All I could think about was that bandana and how it was going to choke to death my boy's dreams of college and a bright future.

In the morning Tomás was still angry with me for going into his room. He yelled, "You can't tell me what to do!" Then he slammed the door. I was terrified that Tomás had already become a member of the local gang.

Gang life is a hard life. I've heard of young men—even one of my own cousins—who think they'll have power if they join. Most of the time the gangs talk to kids around Tomás's age, when they're still little boys. The boys see how "well" the leaders live and want to be a part of it. But these little kids don't know what's in store for them.

In order to be a member, they tell the boys, they must first pass a test. Sometimes the leaders ask the boys to steal something, like a car, or do something violent, like hurt a rival gang member. Other times the initiation is called "jumping in," and the boy gets attacked by all the other gang members. If he doesn't show pain or emotion as he's being beaten up, he passes.

I can't stand the idea of Tomás's hurting others or being hurt. I don't know how I can stop him from becoming a member if he really wants to. But there are some things I can do, and I've told Tomás I am determined to do them.

The first thing I will do is to call the police if I think my son is involved with violence. I have a friend whose son brought guns and even an AK-47 into her home, but she was too afraid to call 911. I told Tomás I am not afraid.

The other thing I plan to do is to imagine Tomás with his guardian angel watching over him at all times. My son may not want an angel, but he's got one. He says he doesn't believe in them; angels are for women. But I tell him his angel was put there by God and there's nothing he can do about it. The angel protects him but also reminds Tomás when he is doing wrong things.

It's been several months since the day I found that bandana. So far my son is still in school and comes home at night. He even told me he's sorry for what he said to me that day. But I know the gangs are hard to resist; they don't give up easily, and once you have joined them, my cousin says, it is nearly impossible to get out. I can only hope my son will remember that he is the one who can bring honor to our family.

Tomás refuses to tell me whether he has joined the gang or not. He says it isn't my business—and in a way, I think it is between him and God. Tomás must decide what kind of life he will choose, and I pray he's just going through a phase—a wannabe. It's hard to let go, but I sleep better at night knowing his angel is watching out for him.

Love grows best in the soil of liberty.

ANONYMOUS

On His Own

Have you ever wondered how the mother of the prodigal son described in the Bible might have felt when her son asked his father for his inheritance and then took off? Scripture doesn't mention the prodigal's mom, but can you imagine her reaction? In the following (obviously fictional) story, we'll sneak a glimpse into what might've been and see how "Abigail" might have reacted to this family crisis.

My husband, Nathan, is a good man, a fair man, a generous man…but when our youngest son, Michael, asked him for his inheritance, I felt certain that Nathan would say, "No, absolutely not!" I ask you, why in the world should my husband give Michael his inheritance? I mean, the boy is barely a man; his beard is still sparse and thin. And even though I'm devoted to my son, I'll be the first to admit that Michael is—well, let's just say he's a little irresponsible. Now, my older son, Jonathan, is the reliable one. He works like an ox, saves every shekel, and never touches strong drink—he's the son who could be trusted with his inheritance.

But don't get me wrong, I love Michael dearly. To be honest, he's probably my favorite. Since his boyhood days he's always been full of spunk and spark. And he's a good musician too, always the center of attention at any social gathering. Perhaps this is partly why I became so angry with Nathan when he agreed to Michael's harebrained

scheme. Giving a kid money like that to go off and do with it whatever he wished? What could come of that but ruin? Did Nathan listen
to me, his devoted wife of twenty-eight years? Ha, think again!

Well, I bade Michael farewell from the step. I put on a tough
front and told him he'd better make good and not bring shame to his
family. But underneath it all I was dying. Anxiety ripped through my
heart like a dull knife. I'm no fool. I know it's a hard, cruel world out
there—it can eat a man alive. I worried that Michael wasn't strong
enough (in body or spirit) to make it on his own. I feared for his
health, his welfare, his very life. But Michael's a stubborn one. And he
walked away from the farm that morning with the proud assurance of
a young bull (a bull that's headed straight for the slaughterhouse!).
But I just bit my lip and waved as I silently begged Jehovah to watch
over my willful boy.

Things sure quieted down in our household after Michael left.
Jonathan continued working harder than ever on the farm. I think it
was partly to impress his father and partly because there was more to
do now that his brother was gone. And I suspected Jonathan resented
Michael for leaving. Perhaps he was envious of his freedom—or the
fact that his younger brother wasn't afraid to go out and try something new. But Jonathan's attitude seemed to harden a little each day.

And I know I didn't help things much. I'm sure I must've walked
around with a pretty big chip on my shoulder. To be honest, I was
absolutely furious at Nathan for having allowed this whole thing to
happen. If he had held back Michael's inheritance until Michael was
older, he still would have been with us—at home—where I felt certain he belonged.

Finally, one evening when Nathan had been unusually quiet, I could no longer contain my thoughts. "Why did you do this, foolish old man?" I yelled. "You should know that Michael's not old enough for such responsibilities!"

Nathan eyed me evenly, then calmly said, "To become a man, Michael must take responsibility for his own life and his own choices. It was Michael's choice to do this thing, and I only gave him what was his. What he does with it is up to him."

"But what if he messes up?" I demanded. "What if he ruins his life? What then?"

"Then we'll see." Nathan stood up and left the room.

Well, rumors started to drift our way. First my cousin Rachel reported having seen Michael in a nearby town "with two questionable women...one on each arm," she whispered with raised brows. Then we heard he was living like royalty—eating and drinking and throwing lavish parties. When Nathan heard this news, he walked out the front door without saying a word and headed directly toward the east field. He didn't return home until long after dark. I could tell he was hurting inside, probably even more than I. But was he angry or worried or just plain sorry? During all those long months, Nathan never spoke a harsh word against his son. You see, my husband has better self-control than I.

Finally, about a year later, I heard Nathan suddenly shout, "He's come back!" And he ran down the dusty road toward a slow-moving, thin silhouette. I peered out into the bright afternoon sun. Could that really be my Michael? And if so, what would his father say? I hurried out to see. And to my happy surprise, Nathan threw his arms open wide and gathered up our boy. "Welcome home, my son!" cried Nathan.

Michael looked worse than a beggar, and he told his father he was truly sorry and would be glad to work like a hired hand on the farm just for something to eat.

"Nonsense," declared Nathan. "You are my son who was lost— and now you are found! We're going to celebrate." Then Nathan turned to me, "Tell the servants to prepare the best fatted calf for our welcome-home dinner!" And so we had a big party.

Now, I'd like to say everything's been just peachy around our place since then, but Jonathan is still jealous over his younger brother's irresponsible escapades. And I wouldn't be surprised if Jonathan doesn't try to pull the same stunt before Passover next spring. But even if he does, I'm sure his father would welcome him back too, with the same open arms and a joyous heart.

If I've learned anything, it's that if you let your young men go, Jehovah God goes with them. Even if they make terrible mistakes on their journey, they can end up the better for them. And, eventually, God can bring them home again.

Letting Go

MELODY

Maybe if I try hard enough
Pray well enough
Hold on tight enough,
Maybe I can keep my child from falling,
Bumbling, tumbling, stumbling
Down, down, down…
Surely, I can protect him from his pain,
Can't I, God?

One by one you pry my frozen fingers loose
From their death-grip grasp,
Yet my fists clench,
My jaw tightens.
I cannot surrender him,
I cannot give him up
Completely,
Can I, God?

I cry out to you—
How can you understand my pain?
Have you ever been a mother?
Do you know how to let go of a son?
Oh, God—

You have...
You do...
Show me.
I inhale your breath of faith,
Trusting you to catch me
And my son
As I relinquish this hold and
Let go.
He's yours, God.
He always was.
I just didn't know it yet.

Into Your Care

Dear heavenly Father,
As an act of trust and worship, I put my son's life in your strong hands today.

Like Hannah, who came back to the temple to give her long-awaited son, Samuel, into the Lord's service, I give back to you the child I want most to keep.

Like Mary, who was chosen for a motherhood of humiliation and grief as well as miracles and wonder, I say to you, "I am the Lord's servant.... May it be to me as you have said" (Luke 1:38, NIV).

As you know better than anyone, Father, I have tried to relinquish my son so many times before. But today I ask for a special measure of grace. Help me to cease all anxious striving, all sinful doubting, and simply release him into your care. Because I am only a mom, and you are a loving and strong and faithful God.

Amen.

I'LL NEVER GIVE UP HOPE

LINDA

The first time Chris ran away the school secretary called, saying he was nowhere to be found. His fourth-grade teacher and classmates searched the playground, the bathrooms, and the library for my son, but he had disappeared. The janitor opened all the broom closets. After an hour Chris was still missing. The secretary wanted to know if I wanted her to call the police.

I told her yes and to alert the national guard if necessary. I'd be right over. Panic choked me, but as I raced out the door, I tried to pray.

For several years I'd been praying that Chris would suddenly grow out of his anxiety problems. One morning I'd wake up and he'd be cured of the temper tantrums, paranoia, and irrational fears that tormented him daily. Someday he'd proudly walk into his class at school with his head held high. I thought I just needed to find the right words—hit on the ultimate prayer formula. Why had my petitions gone unanswered? Perhaps I wasn't praying hard enough.

As I opened the car door, I squeezed my eyes shut, wordlessly mouthing an emergency plea for Chris's safety. Then I heard a small sniffle coming from behind a cardboard box in our garage. I found my little boy huddled on the concrete, crying softly. We prayed together, and I told him neither God nor I would ever give up on him. Chris smiled and looked relieved. But the next day he did the same thing again.

By sixth grade he refused to attend school. Every day was a battle. My husband and I had read a book about discipline that suggested we force our son to class by carrying him if necessary. My husband enlisted the help of a very tall friend, and one day the two men hauled Chris, kicking and cursing, into the middle school. The incident was disastrous for all of us. And panic attacks and anxiety continued to be a problem for our son.

Over the years we've learned that Chris is not your run-of-the-mill teenager, the sort that just needs a swift kick in the pants to get going in school or in life. That might work for his two brothers, but Chris isn't going to straighten up and fly right with stricter discipline or one of those "tough love" boot camps. Chris is different.

Maybe your son is different too. Maybe he's got attention deficit disorder (ADD) or a learning disorder that makes school difficult— for him and for you. Or your son has been given a clinical diagnosis of mental illness, like bipolar disorder or even schizophrenia. Maybe the doctors are stumped and just don't know what's going on with your son.

This uncertainty is probably the greatest test of our faith as moms of lost boys. After years of going through our sons' trials, we're unsure whether they will ever improve. We wonder if they'll grow up to lead normal lives. Deep down we know there is no ultimate prayer formula that will magically make things better. And yet we can't give up hope.

The apostle Paul said, "And hope does not disappoint us, because God has poured out his love into our hearts by the Holy Spirit, whom he has given us" (Romans 5:5, NIV). In order to stay in hope rather than disappointment, I am trying to stop praying that Chris will be the son I once imagined and instead to ask for the boy God wants him to be. I want to collect a whole new set of hopes to get me through each day.

Some of these hopes will be for myself. Hope that I'll learn to work with Chris in the best way for him. Hope that I'll stay calm even when his behavior infuriates me. Hope that I'll hang in there when things seem hopeless.

Some things I hope for him. I hope that he'll learn to function independently as an adult. I hope that he'll turn his eyes toward God when he feels trapped and alone. Most of all I hope he'll always believe I love him.

We still don't have a diagnosis for our son, although Chris is nearly twenty now. The path we've walked may be all too familiar to you. You've taken your lost boy to psychiatrists and counselors. You've been to family social workers, tried drug therapy. Maybe you've even let him get into a scrape with the law to "get him help through the system," as professionals say. Nothing has helped, and at times perhaps your faith has been stretched far beyond what you thought possible. Still…you don't give up on your son.

We may have terrible days, and in moments of crisis we may claim we can't take it anymore. Yet even when things are so bad that we're past tears, it's still possible to pray. No matter how much we hurt, each day we can pick a fresh bouquet of hope. It's the one thing that never disappoints.

═══════

Hope begins in the dark,
the stubborn hope that if you just show up
and try to do the right thing,
the dawn will come.
You wait and watch and work:
you don't give up.

ANNE LAMOTT

Darkest Hour

Sharista knew that her son Jamal had problems. Serious problems. But he was twenty and living on his own. And in a last attempt to save her marriage, she'd been trying to cut the apron strings with him. Yet her heart wasn't ready to give up. The mother in her said that perhaps her son could still be saved—if she could just hold on to hope.

I felt caught between a rock and a hard place. Jamal, my youngest child, had been plagued with trouble throughout high school, but somehow he managed to graduate and get accepted into college. However, he dropped out after the first term. Off and on, he'd live at home, sometimes working, sometimes not. This went on until last year when his father told him it was time to move out.

My husband is what he calls a "self-made man"—and proud of it. It's not easy being African-American in a predominantly white town, and sometimes I think James is overly concerned about what others think of him and his family. And yet I was afraid he might be right about Jamal. At the same time I worried that Jamal wasn't ready yet. I didn't think he could make it on his own. But our marriage was suffering, and having our son there only made things worse. It seemed that Jamal and James fought constantly, and I always felt trapped in the middle.

"He'll never know what the real world's like if you keep protecting him," James insisted. I finally gave in. But even so, I took time off from my job and helped Jamal find a place to live. I cosigned the rental agreement with him and loaned him money. I even gave him all kinds of things to set up housekeeping. "You're making it too easy on him," my husband complained. But I couldn't help myself. I already felt so mean for making him move out of our large, comfortable home with four bedrooms just sitting empty. His low-paying job would barely cover his rent and utilities, not to mention food. I made a secret plan to stop by now and then to drop off groceries—and to check on him.

Our two older daughters had been on their own for some time now, but even they were split on the Jamal issue. The oldest one, Kiesha, thought we were being too hard on him. "He's just a late bloomer," she said. "He just needs time to find himself." But Lana agreed with her dad, saying, "Jamal will never become responsible if you don't make him."

I still wasn't sure what I thought. I hoped this move was what he needed. I hoped it would make him stronger. If nothing else, I hoped that he might even decide that going to college was better than living hand-to-mouth in that crummy little apartment.

About three weeks passed, and Jamal seemed to be getting along okay. I worried that he wasn't eating well, but at least he still had his job and seemed to be hanging in there. I started to feel more hopeful that this had been the right decision. Although, to be perfectly honest, it had made no difference in our marriage. Things between James and me seemed the same as ever. It's not that I don't love my husband.

I do. And the almost thirty years we've been together are important to me. I figured that maybe I just wasn't trying hard enough. I even went to see counselor for help.

Then one night, about a month after Jamal's move, we got a phone call. Jamal was being treated in the emergency room. He'd attempted to kill himself with an overdose of over-the-counter sleeping pills.

Frantic, James and I raced to the hospital. I said nothing during the drive, but I kept thinking this was all James's fault. He'd forced Jamal to move out before he was ready. I knew if our son didn't make it, I would hold it against James—maybe forever.

Jamal was still unconscious when we arrived. We learned that he had made the 911 call himself. "He probably changed his mind," said the nurse in a matter-of-fact voice, as if this were a common occurrence in the ER (which I suppose it was). Finally they finished the last stomach pumping and administered medication to counteract the effect of the sleeping pills, and one of us was allowed to go and sit with Jamal. I insisted, and James didn't argue.

It was the longest night of my life. The doctor said they were waiting for Jamal to respond now. If he would. He told me to go ahead and talk with Jamal and try to stimulate some sort of reaction. And so I just chattered away at my son. I talked about how happy I'd been when he'd been born. How his baby smile was like a sunny day. I talked about his first wobbly steps. And about the time he'd pulled out all the carrot seedlings just to see what they looked like underneath.

I tried not to notice the hollows of his bronze cheeks or the several days' worth of stubble that grew on his chin. Instead, I rambled on about his grade-school days and how he'd been the best speller in second grade. On and on, going over each year of his life like an old movie. Even when I hit his troubled high-school days, I managed to come up with things he'd done that I'd been proud of, like the time he'd stood up for a friend and gotten himself into trouble or when he'd performed community service, donating twenty extra hours just because he thought it was a good cause.

Suddenly the troubles he'd had as a teen no longer seemed so terrible. And I wondered what all the fuss had been about. "Maybe we expected too much from you," I said with tears now choking my voice. "Maybe we forgot to tell you just how wonderful you really are. How much we love you. How proud we are of you." I continued talking, but I can't remember what else I said. I just kept on, hoping that somehow my string of words would be like a lifeline for him to grab on to.

Finally I realized that I was no longer talking to Jamal. I was praying—begging and pleading with God to spare my son's life.

And finally, at about four in the morning, Jamal came to. His deep brown eyes had never looked so sad as he apologized. "I know it was stupid, Mom. Right after I did it, I knew it was a big mistake." I told him not to worry about it just then. I told him everything would be all right, that we'd find him help. "You've got your family behind you," I told him.

"What about Dad?" he asked with a troubled brow.

"Don't worry about Dad," I told him. But when I finally made it back to James and assured him that Jamal was going to be okay, he got really mad.

"I can't believe he pulled such a crazy stunt," James fumed. "Does he think this is going to get him back into the house?"

I couldn't believe what I was hearing. I just turned and walked away. Suddenly I felt I was going to have to choose between my husband and my son. And whether it was right or wrong, I chose my son. It was all I could do.

James and I are separated for the time being. Jamal and I live in a bigger, nicer apartment. He's got a better job, is taking antidepressants, and is getting regular counseling at our church. And he plans to return to college next year. I told James that I'm willing to go to a marriage counselor with him, with possibly some family counseling later on (I see now where we've both made mistakes), and he's considering it. I'm still not positive I made the right decision, and I can't say this has all been easy. But I know I made the only choice I could. And for that I'm not sorry.

Perhaps in time our family will reunite. For now, Jamal needs me, and I'm committed to seeing him through this.

<hr>

Now faith is the substance of things hoped for,
the evidence of things not seen.

HEBREWS 11:1

Building a Prayer Altar

W hen your son is in a lot of trouble, what often helps most is praying. Some moms find it helpful to build a prayer altar to remind them to pray—and to trust God. Each person's prayer altar should be unique, her own, but here are some suggestions for putting one together:

Placement: You may want it to be private, in your bedroom or somewhere others won't ask questions. Some moms, however, choose to have their altar out where everyone will see it—including their son. All you need is some bare space on a counter or small table. Make sure it's a place you'll feel comfortable getting on your knees or in whatever posture you like to pray.

Pictures: If you have a picture of Jesus or some plaque that has spiritual significance to you, place that on the altar. Include a picture of your son when was little, as well as a picture of him now.

God's Word: Placing a Bible at your altar will remind you, first of all, to open it, read it, and listen to what God might say to you through his Word. It also symbolizes your trust in God, in his promises, and that what he's said is true.

Candles: Lighting a candle is something Christians have been doing for many years to remind them of the light that Jesus brings. Using some inexpensive, utilitarian candles (or some more lavish and personal, if you wish), you can make use of the hope and beauty candles emanate.

Pray at your prayer altar at least once a day, and let its presence remind you in the meantime that you have placed your son in God's loving care.

Always Another Program

Brandon, eighteen, is Liz's only child. He's had learning problems since he was young and was diagnosed with attention deficit disorder in middle school. Since elementary school, Brandon has seen counselors, psychologists, psychiatrists, and behavioral specialists. He's been enrolled in dozens of special schools and programs. Brandon usually does well at first, but within weeks he gets kicked out or refuses to attend whatever program Liz finds for him. Liz keeps looking for new programs for her son, never giving up hope that he'll find success.

When Brandon was diagnosed with attention deficit disorder at age twelve, I thought our troubles were over. Medication, patience, and a special school would fix my son. I'm a former special ed teacher. I was certain I'd find a great program for my son.

Brandon's a good-looking kid—his wide smile and dark eyes can light up a room. He's rather shy and has a soft voice. He'd rather draw pictures than work on cars. Getting along with Brandon has been difficult for his stepfather, John, who works as a mechanic and loves fixing things.

John has complained that I put too much stock in books and experts—he thought Brandon needed tougher discipline to get him to behave. "The kid just needs somebody to yank his chain," John has said more than once. I thought I knew better though—my training in learning disorders gave me an advantage.

Brandon's behavior at school was typical of kids with ADD. His short attention span made it hard for him to follow a string of instructions, and he often forgot what he'd learned the hour before. Then he'd get embarrassed and act out in class. In seventh grade Brandon spent more time in the hall or at the principal's office than he did at his desk. The teachers would tell me that he was a sweet kid, not mean, but he was often disruptive.

I finally enrolled him in a school that specialized in behavior modification. They gave out M&Ms when the kids stayed on task. The students were almost all boys. Many also had emotional problems or had been in serious trouble with the law. It was really scary to take Brandon there. Some of the boys were arsonists or hardcore gang members. Brandon lasted about two weeks before he begged me to find an alternative.

My next strategy was to move out into the country. I thought if we were in a rural setting with smaller schools, Brandon would be away from city problems and would receive more individual help. Brandon didn't want to leave his friends, but we relocated in a farming community. I enrolled him in the local school.

In the meantime my husband and I drove twenty miles into town for our jobs plus all of Brandon's appointments. I took him to vision therapy and developmental therapy every week. I also had Brandon see a psychiatrist because, in addition to the attention problems, he was now doing bizarre things like eating paint in class. I had EEGs done to see if there was anything wrong with his brain waves. No diagnosis except for the ADD ever showed up. And then I got a call from the rural school.

Brandon had been suspended for using a racial slur against another student. I couldn't believe it. He denied it, but since he was failing all his classes anyway, I transferred him to another school a few miles away. The new school was willing to let Brandon work on an IEP (Individual Education Program), and he liked the school better because it was closer to town.

I should have guessed that if he got closer to town, he'd skip school. After a few weeks I found out that after being dropped off, Brandon was taking a city bus to town and spending his days just hanging out. In the afternoons he'd make it back to the school in time to be picked up. I was furious, and his stepfather threatened to send him to one of those juvenile boot camps in the desert.

Brandon threatened to run away if we sent him to boarding school. He was seventeen by now—not cooperating with anything. He managed to stay out of trouble with the law, but he was no closer to finishing school than he'd been at fourteen. I decided my only option was to quit my job and homeschool my son.

Homeschooling was a joke. Here I was, a certified special ed teacher, and I couldn't get Brandon to study. He always had an excuse. He'd stayed up too late, or he wasn't feeling well. We took away privileges, allowance, but there wasn't that much more we could withhold. He didn't want to learn how to drive, so a driver's license or car didn't mean that much. When we removed his television, stereo, and computer privileges, he drew pictures or played his guitar. If we said he couldn't go out, he'd sleep so much that I began to worry.

By the time I got Brandon enrolled in a GED preparation class at the local community college, I wondered if he would remember anything he'd ever learned. John and I really sat on Brandon that year, forcing him to stick with it. The GED class was individualized, so he was able to get a lot of help. Even though he failed several of the GED tests, we kept after him until he passed. We held a graduation party last spring in his honor, and I've never seen his smile so wide.

Getting his GED has increased Brandon's confidence. He knows he can be successful. But being in so many individualized and special programs has left him without some important social skills. Finding and keeping a job has been tough. He's learned the hard way that employers have strict requirements and that ADD no longer excuses him.

So Brandon is in another program, where they teach him job skills and take him to interviews. I don't know yet if this program will help my son, but he says he's determined to hang in there. No matter what happens, I want Brandon to know one thing for sure: I'll never give up on him.

Kiss the Kids

Kyra and Peter used to make their home in Springfield, Oregon, where her children attended school with Kip Kinkle, the boy responsible for the Thurston High School shootings in 1998. The tragedy gave Kyra a renewed ability to appreciate the trials and problems associated with raising teenage boys. It also made her realize how much we all need to pray for moms who have "lost boys."

R ecently my son's high school received a bomb threat. We quickly learned that this was just one of hundreds of bogus bomb scares that have taken place around the country in recent years. But this was different. *This was my son's school.*

My heart sank as Tracey, sixteen, related to me how officials spent two hours moving the kids out into the cold, herding them from one field to another, until they finally cancelled the day's classes and sent everyone home. After he told me about it (and how great it was that he missed a test in science as a result), we proceeded to have a conversation so unanticipated it seemed surreal.

"I want you to be really, really careful at school, Tracey," I told him. *Not in a football game, not at a party, not driving in your car...but at school!*

"Careful of what?" he said.

"I don't know exactly," I said. "Other boys, I guess. Boys who seem off-kilter."

"Yeah," he answered, "we have a few of those kind at school."

"You do? Well, be nice to them!" I said. "Promise me. I'm serious!"

He rolled his eyes. "Whatever, Mom."

No wonder this warning sounded strange to Tracey. In recent months we'd had problems with him that required warnings much more threatening than this one. My husband and I had discovered that Tracey had been smoking pot almost daily for the past year. We got him into counseling, but now I worried constantly about what could happen if he continued to abuse drugs.

I realized with a jolt how this problem with pot was so minor in comparison to what could happen. I was reminded again of the shootings at Thurston High School and how close to home they'd felt. Our family had lived in Springfield for ten years. My kids attended Thurston Elementary and Thurston Middle School, and I'd planned for Tracey to attend high school there. (Thurston was the "good" high school in town). The shooter, Kip Kinkle, was on Tracey's soccer team, which I coached for two years. I remember him as a cute, wily, freckle-faced kid who could dribble the ball better than anyone on the team. I think he played right wing.

Remembering Kip and the boys he eventually killed, I felt a familiar pang of guilt. You know, the one where you wonder, *Why them and not me? Why does it take another parent's loss to make me realize my richness? And why on earth don't I lie down every night and wake up every morning praising God that my children are alive—able to argue over curfews, accidentally swear in my presence, and squirm out of my arms when I hug them too long?*

I considered some of the things I'd been fretting over lately. My twelve-year-old son, Jamie, won't stop leaving his wet towel on the bathroom floor. He keeps breaking important parts on his braces, and he rarely gets out the door to school on time. Tracey, meanwhile, in addition to his dope problem, is not studying hard enough to get into his choice of colleges.

Such precious, wonderful problems! Such glorious, hopeful problems!

Like so many others, while the tragedy at Thurston was unfolding, I found myself glued to the television. At one point in the coverage, I remember that a reporter with no new developments to announce mentioned he'd just overheard a shaken policeman at the scene calling home. "Kiss the kids," he'd told his wife. "Go kiss the kids."

Somehow, out of all the hours of news I'd watched years before—footage of tear-streaked faces, agonized officials, parents running across the lawn in terror—this is what I remember most to this day. "Kiss the kids."

And lately I've been realizing why. For those of us mothers who still have our children, this may be all we can give to those who don't. We owe it to them to remember—to really see and enjoy and connect with our teenagers. To delight in every sweaty hug or unexpected smile. To endure patiently—and hopefully—every painful problem, dark mood, stupid choice, and even some very bad, very loud music.

We owe it to them—and to ourselves—to kiss our kids as often as possible and to pray in earnest for those moms who no longer can.

Stain Remover

LINDA

I tried
to give your shirt away—
the one smeared with ketchup
and French fry grease,
spattered with spray paint and tears.

I tossed
your old favorite to the rag bag,
but you always rescued it,
hugged it close,
scolded me for giving up too soon.

I Shouted
out stains as best I could,
fluff-dried a shirt as sorry as
some of your predicaments:
dangerously thin.

I smiled—
at how you brightened,
how you love that shirt
the same eternal way
God and I love you.

Prayer Champion

Dear God,

In the midst of the challenges we face in our family, you invite me to be a prayer champion for my son. I accept this invitation with fresh purpose today. And with Jesus' disciples, I ask, "Lord, teach [me] to pray."

Teach me to pray always. Teach me to come with a clean heart, humility, and pure motives. Teach me to be persistent. Teach me to be honest, to be bold, to be thankful. Teach me to be still and listen to you.

Thank you for this important ministry of intercession. May I be a faithful prayer champion for my children, because Jesus promised, "Ask and it will be given to you; seek and you will find; knock and the door will be opened to you. For everyone who asks receives; he who seeks finds; and to him who knocks, the door will be opened" (Matthew 7:7-8, NIV).

In Jesus' name, amen.